The Problem of Globalisation

ISSUES

Volume 157

Series Editor

Lisa Firth

Independence

Educational Publishers
Cambridge

First published by Independence
The Studio, High Green
Great Shelford
Cambridge CB22 5EG
England

© Independence 2008

British Library Cataloguing in Publication Data
The Problem of Globalisation – (Issues Series)
I. Firth, Lisa II. Series
303.4'82

ISBN 978 1 86168 444 8

Printed in Great Britain
MWL Print Group Ltd

Cover
The illustration on the front cover is by
Simon Kneebone.

CONTENTS

Chapter One: Overview

Chapter Two: Globalisation and Trade

00094067490010

Useful information for readers

Dear Reader,

Issues: The Problem of Globalisation

Thanks to increasing foreign travel and the growth of the internet, the world today seems like a much smaller place. However, the 'global village' is not without disadvantages. Some say increased trade has allowed large corporations to take advantage of workers in developing countries, over 1 billion of whom still work for less than $1 a day. Others believe, however, that free trade is economically necessary. This title looks at the debate surrounding the rise of globalisation.

The purpose of *Issues*

The Problem of Globalisation is the one hundred and fifty-seventh volume in the **Issues** series. The aim of this series is to offer up-to-date information about important issues in our world. Whether you are a regular reader or new to the series, we do hope you find this book a useful overview of the many and complex issues involved in the topic.

Titles in the **Issues** series are resource books designed to be of especial use to those undertaking project work or requiring an overview of facts, opinions and information on a particular subject, particularly as a prelude to undertaking their own research.

The information in this book is not from a single author, publication or organisation; the value of this unique series lies in the fact that it presents information from a wide variety of sources, including:

⇨ Government reports and statistics
⇨ Newspaper articles and features
⇨ Information from think-tanks and policy institutes
⇨ Magazine features and surveys
⇨ Website material
⇨ Literature from lobby groups and charitable organisations. *

Critical evaluation

Because the information reprinted here is from a number of different sources, readers should bear in mind the origin of the text and whether the source is likely to have a particular bias or agenda when presenting information (just as they would if undertaking their own research). It is hoped that, as you read about the many aspects of the issues explored in this book, you will critically evaluate the information presented. It is important that you decide whether you are being presented with facts or opinions. Does the writer give a biased or an unbiased report? If an opinion is being expressed, do you agree with the writer?

The Problem of Globalisation offers a useful starting point for those who need convenient access to information about the many issues involved. However, it is only a starting point. Following each article is a URL to the relevant organisation's website, which you may wish to visit for further information.

Kind regards,

Lisa Firth
Editor, **Issues** series

* Please note that Independence Publishers has no political affiliations or opinions on the topics covered in the Issues series, and any views quoted in this book are not necessarily those of the publisher or its staff.

ISSUES TODAY
A RESOURCE FOR KEY STAGE 3

Younger readers can also now benefit from the thorough editorial process which characterises the **Issues** series with the launch of a new range of titles for 11- to 14-year-old students, **Issues Today**. In addition to containing information from a wide range of sources, rewritten with this age group in mind, **Issues Today** titles also feature comprehensive glossaries, an accessible and attractive layout and handy tasks and assignments which can be used in class, for homework or as a revision aid. In addition, these titles are fully photocopiable. For more information, please visit the **Issues Today** section of our website (www.independence. co.uk).

What is globalisation?

Information from the Foreign and Commonwealth Office

Globalisation is an imprecise term covering many aspects of politics, economics and culture. Its origins are complex and virtually every one of the 2822 academic papers and 589 new books on globalisation written in 1998 would include their own definition. However, most writers would agree it is a process driven by technological change and rapid advances in communications.

Globalisation leads to greater interdependence between countries as goods, services, capital, labour, knowledge and information move increasingly quickly and freely around the world. Aspects of globalisation include international trade and investment, international agreements to protect the world environment and growth in the number and scope of international organisations.

Whilst globalisation presents opportunities for all countries it is clear that some countries have benefited more than others. The challenge is to ensure that the process is more equitable and more sustainable. The Foreign and Commonwealth Office is a vigorous champion of Corporate Citizenship and Sustainable Development working with other Governments, NGOs and multinational companies to establish standards for human rights and the environment.

Given the rapid changes associated with globalisation many people have strong concerns about the way in which it impacts on their lives.

What are the potential benefits?

Overall, globalisation should lead to higher rates of economic growth.

International trade promotes efficiency and saves resources by encouraging production of goods and services in countries where the costs are lowest. It leads to lower prices for consumers by creating greater competition between businesses. Trade boosts growth by creating new opportunities through larger markets, creating more jobs, and enabling the specialisation of labour, boosting productivity. Trade between two countries increases economic welfare in both by widening the range of goods and services available for consumption.

The UK economy is benefiting disproportionately from globalisation. We are the world's fourth largest trading nation and second largest foreign investor. Trade represents over 40% of our GDP, twice that of the US or Japan. Inward investment into the UK has created 815,000 jobs to date and accounts for nearly 30% of net manufacturing output. We are particularly strong in business and financial services, telecoms and media – sectors that thrive on globalisation.

Improved governance is another potential benefit of globalisation. Better communications technology, and particularly the Internet, mean governments can more easily be held to account, allowing greater scrutiny of government spending by citizens. This also applies to businesses, enabling better oversight of UK assets overseas. Information technology can also be used to promote innovative programmes and play a key role in the work of environmental, human rights and poverty reduction NGOs.

Another recent development that has helped millions of people is the globalisation of knowledge through information technology. One example is the use of public Internet kiosks in rural India to revolutionise medical treatment and eye care. In the village of Padinettankudi in Tamil Nadu a webcam and online patient questionnaire are being used to photograph and record villagers' eye problems. Once recorded they are then emailed to the specialist Aravind Eye Hospital, affordably reducing to a few seconds a process that would previously have taken days or weeks. An online doctor/patient discussion takes place subsequently before a free appointment is arranged, saving scarce resources and equitably improving health outcomes.

Globalisation can also be seen as a force for stability. Economic integration normally reduces the possibility of armed conflict and has been central to the peaceful relations in Western Europe witnessed in the second half of the 20th century.

Scientific breakthroughs like the mapping of the Human Genome (through co-operation of scientific teams across the globe) and aspects of contemporary life such as a diverse range of foods in UK supermarkets and affordable foreign travel are amongst the many other benefits of globalisation.

⇨ Information from the Foreign and Commonwealth Office. Visit www.fco.gov.uk for more information.

Globalisation explained

Information from the Economic and Social Research Council

Globalisation is a broad umbrella term for modern international interrelationships, but in the past academic research has tried to pin down a definition of the complex web of processes and activities contained in the term 'globalisation'.

The sociologist, Anthony Giddens, has described it as a 'decoupling of space and time'. Professor Jan Aart Scholte, co-director of the ESRC-funded Centre for the Study of Globalisation and Regionalisation at the University of Warwick, sees it as 'the spread of transplanetary – and in recent times more supraterritorial – connections between people'.

Facts

⇨ Global income is more than $40.2 trillion a year, but 19 per cent (1.21 billion) of the world's population earn less than $1 a day [1] [2].

⇨ 84 per cent of the global population earns only 20 per cent of global income, and within many countries there is a large gap between rich and poor that is growing [1].

⇨ Between 1990 and 2004 the sum of merchandise exports and imports in low income countries rose from 24.1 per cent of GDP to 37.8 per cent of GDP. This

growing financial integration with the global economy has helped reduce poverty in many countries and this results in longer life expectancy, lower mortality rates and improved schooling [3].

⇨ Sea level rise, warming temperatures, uncertain effects on forest and agricultural systems, and increased variability and volatility in weather patterns are expected to have a significant and disproportionate impact in the developing world, where the world's poor remain most susceptible to the potential damages and uncertainties inherent in a changing climate [4].

⇨ The digital and information revolution has changed the way the world learns, communicates, does business and treats illnesses. In 2004, there were 545 people per 1000 using the internet in

high income countries, while there were only 24 per 1000 in low income countries [5].

Types of globalisation

There are varying processes of globalisation which can be placed into four areas.

⇨ Economic globalisation, including industrial and financial globalisation, encompasses the rise and expansion of multinational enterprises and the emergence of worldwide financial markets and better access to external financing for corporate, national and sub national borrowers.

---

84 per cent of the global population earns only 20 per cent of global income

---

⇨ Political and military globalisation refers to the spread of political interests to the regions and countries outside the neighbourhood of political (state and non-state) actors and long-distance networks of interdependence in which force, and the threat or promise of force are employed.

⇨ Social and cultural globalisation involves the movement of ideas, information, images and people around the globe.

⇨ Environmental globalisation refers to the long-distance transport of materials in the atmosphere or oceans, or it can relate to the biological substances such as pathogens or genetic materials. Examples include the spread of the HIV virus and the effects of ozone-depleting chemicals.

The World Trade Organisation

The World Trade Organisation (WTO) is the only international organisation dealing with the global

rules of trade between nations. Its main function is to ensure that trade flows as smoothly, predictably and freely as possible. It was set up in 1995 to succeed the General Agreement on Tariffs and Trade (GATT) established in the wake of the Second World War. It currently has 150 member countries.

The director-general of WTO is Pascal Lamy, former EU trade commissioner, whose stated aim is to open channels of trade, promote growth and development, improve the standards of living and reduce global poverty.

The Doha Development Agenda was launched in 2001 and aims to lower trade barriers for developing countries, but negotiations have stalled over disputes between developed nations and the major developing nations.

The issues and perceived effects of globalisation excite strong feelings, tempting people to regard it in terms of black and white. Supporters of the WTO say it is democratic, and that by expanding world trade, the WTO helps to raise living standards around the world.

Critics of globalisation, such as WTO Watch and Global Trade Watch, present it as the 'worldwide drive toward a globalised economic system

dominated by supranational corporate trade and banking institutions that are not accountable to democratic processes or national governments'. They argue that the WTO is too powerful, is run by the rich for the rich and is indifferent to the wider impact of free trade and that the social and environmental costs are borne by the public. They also say that the WTO lacks democratic accountability because its hearings on trade disputes are closed to the public and the media.

Understanding globalisation

There is an enormous interest in the effects of, and implications of globalisation and regionalisation. The central task of the Centre for Globalisation and Regionalisation at Warwick is understanding, defining and explaining globalisation – be it in its economic, political, socio-cultural and historical guises – and where possible, measuring and quantifying it using the CSGR Globalisation Index.

The ESRC Warwick Centre is the only purpose-designated centre dealing in a comprehensive manner with globalisation and its linkages with regionalisation. The centre provides both a national and international site for interaction between scholars

and practitioners (from both the public and private sector). Its target community and audience are global, rather than national.

Notes

1 Size of the economy (2006) World Development Indicators, The World Bank Group, Table 1.1 (Accessed 14 February 2007)
2 Millennium Development Goals Report (2006) United Nations Millennium Project, p 4 (Accessed 14 February 2007)
3 Integration with the global economy (2006) World Development Indicators, The World Bank Group, Table 6.1 (Accessed 14 February 2007)
4 Potential outcome (2006) Woods Hole Research Centre (accessed 12 February 2007)
5 The information age (2006) World Development Indicators, The World Bank Group, Table 5.10 (Accessed 14 February 2007)
Updated 17 August 2007

⇨ The above information is reprinted with kind permission from the Economic and Social Research Council. Visit www.esrcsocietytoday. ac.uk for more information on this and related issues.

© ESRC

Globalisation defined

Information from the Trades Union Congress

Globalisation is a term that is frequently used but seldom defined. It refers to the rapid increase in the share of economic activity taking place across national boundaries.

This goes beyond the international trade in goods and includes the way those goods are produced, the delivery and sale of services, and the movement of capital.

Threat or opportunity

Globalisation can be a force for good. It has the potential to generate wealth and improve living standards. But it isn't doing that well at the moment.

The benefits from increased trade, investment, and technological innovation are not fairly distributed. The experience of the international trade union movement suggests that the reality for the majority of the world's population is that things are getting worse.

Globalisation as we know it is increasing the gap between rich and poor. This is because the policies that drive the globalisation process are largely focused on the needs of business.

The relentless drive to

liberalise trade, i.e. to remove trade barriers, promote privatisation, and reduce regulation (including legal protection for workers), has had a negative impact on the lives of millions of people around the world. In addition, many of the poorer countries have been pressured to orientate their economies towards producing exports and to reduce already inadequate spending on public services such as health and education so that they can repay their foreign debt. This has forced even more people into a life of poverty and uncertainty.

The role of governments

The type of globalisation we are experiencing is sometimes portrayed as an inevitable, technologically driven process that we must adapt to in order to survive and prosper. For millions of workers, in the developing as well as the developed world, this has been translated into living with greater job insecurity and worse conditions.

> **The type of globalisation we are experiencing is sometimes portrayed as an inevitable, technologically driven process that we must adapt to**

But the reality is that the globalisation we have seen in recent decades has been driven by a laborious process of international rule-making and enforcement. Governments have made those rules. There has been a conscious political choice to pursue the policies that underpin the process. Of course, domestic, economic, industrial and social policies also play a crucial role in determining living conditions, though poorer countries are less able to resist globalisation due to their economically weaker position.

The key players

A number of key players are driving globalisation. They include:
⇨ multinational enterprises which carry out business across national boundaries;
⇨ the World Trade Organisation (WTO), through which international trade agreements are negotiated and enforced;
⇨ the World Bank and the Inter-national Monetary Fund (IMF) which are meant to assist governments in achieving development aims through the provision of loans and technical assistance.

They have championed the trade liberalisation policies mentioned above. Governments, and these international institutions are instrumental in determining the outcome of globalisation.

The impact on women

The impact of globalisation on men and women is different.

Women, particularly those in developing countries, suffer disproportionately when public services are cut back. This is because they have primary responsibility for caring for children and other family members. Also, girls are more likely to be withdrawn from school when the family income needs to be supplemented or when the cost of education rises.

While the expansion of international trade has generated employment opportunities for women in certain circumstances, trade policies have often served to entrench the traditionally inferior role assigned to women in many countries. Occupational segregation, pay inequality, and unequal access to resources are but a few of the discriminatory measures that women face. The rise of Export Processing zones where large numbers of young women labour in poor and dangerous conditions to produce cheap consumer goods, and the expansion of outsourcing and home-based employment have also raised new issues and concerns for women workers.

Putting people first

Ways need to be found to manage and structure globalisation so that it supports fundamental human rights and sustainable development, and generates prosperity for ordinary people, particularly the poorest. Left unchecked, globalisation will lead to their further marginalisation and impoverishment.

⇨ The above information is reprinted with kind permission from the Trades Union Congress. Visit www.tuc.org.uk for more information.
© Trades Union Congress

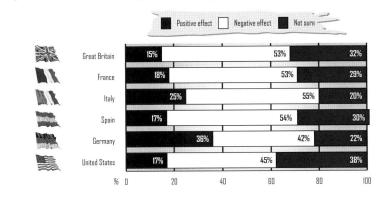

European views of globalisation

Respondents were asked: 'Do you think globalisation is having a positive or negative effect in [your country]?'

Positive effect | Negative effect | Not sure

Country	Positive effect	Negative effect	Not sure
Great Britain	15%	53%	32%
France	18%	53%	29%
Italy	25%	55%	20%
Spain	17%	54%	30%
Germany	36%	42%	22%
United States	17%	45%	38%

% 0   20   40   60   80   100

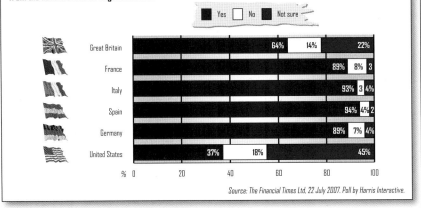

Respondents were asked: 'Should the European Union do more to protect people from the adverse effects of globalisation?'

Yes | No | Not sure

Country	Yes	No	Not sure
Great Britain	64%	14%	22%
France	89%	8%	3
Italy	93%	3	4%
Spain	94%	4%	2
Germany	89%	7%	4%
United States	37%	18%	45%

% 0   20   40   60   80   100

Source: The Financial Times Ltd, 22 July 2007. Poll by Harris Interactive.

A globalisation glossary

An A-Z of short definitions

Bretton Woods. Bretton Woods is the name of the place in the United States where an international meeting was held in 1944, towards the end of the Second World War. The main participants were the United States and Great Britain.

As a result of this meeting the IMF and World Bank were formed, as was the General Agreement on Trade and Tariffs (GATT) and the United Nations. GATT was replaced by the World Trade Organisation (WTO) in 1995.

The IMF, World Bank and WTO are sometimes referred to as the Bretton Woods institutions.

Capital flight. Money taken out of a country by a company or individual to be invested abroad, usually in the hope that it will be safer or make more profit.

Cold War. The Cold War is the name given to the period between the end of the Second World War (1945) and 1991 when the United States of America, representing Capitalism, and the Soviet Union, representing Communism, were 'at war'.

It is called the Cold War because the 'war' was mainly ideological – about ideas – capitalism versus communism. Although there was plenty of 'traditional' fighting it all took place in other countries, such as Vietnam and Afghanistan.

Commercial debt. Debt owed to banks and other companies.

Commodity. Agricultural and/or mineral product produced by a country that can be traded.

Continent/Country. Geographers split the world into continents composed of a number of countries. The most common split is into seven continents: Europe, North America, South America, Africa, Asia, Australia (sometimes called Australasia or Oceania to include New Zealand and some of the Pacific Islands) and Antarctica (which is not a collection of countries).

The Debt Crisis. The story of the most recent debt crisis starts in the 1970s. The Oil Producing Countries (OPEC) joined together and made a big increase in the price of oil, which was traded in US dollars. The result was that dollars flowed into the OPEC countries from all over the world, from all the countries that buy oil. Most First World countries buy oil. The OPEC countries invested the dollars they received in private banks (Barclays, NatWest etc.) in Europe. The banks needed to make a return for their investors (i.e. pay them interest) and so began lending to Third World and in some cases to Socialist countries.

Globalisation is an imprecise term, which is used to define a series of partially interlinked economic, technological, commercial, political, social and cultural processes

---

Some countries wanted to borrow to promote 'debt led growth', others only borrowed to pay for more expensive oil. However, many wasted the money on military equipment and/or allowed the corrupt elites to benefit from currency scams and capital flight – taking the money borrowed out of the country and investing it elsewhere, often in private bank accounts. Many governments at that time were dictatorships and cared little for the poor majority of their population. However, when these countries could not pay their debts it was the poor that suffered as public services and jobs were cut to find money to pay the banks.

In the 1980s interest rates went up at the same time as Third World exports (commodities) lost their value. Several countries declared they were unable to pay their debts. This failure to be able to pay is referred to as 'the debt crisis'.

Food security. Food security exists when all people, at all times, have physical and economic access to sufficient, safe and nutritious food to meet their dietary needs and food requirements for an active and healthy life. Opinions differ on how this should be achieved. Some see it as a technical problem of growing enough food.

Others see it as a political problem and they argue that there is enough food, or at least that people know how to produce enough food, the problem therefore is that the resources needed to buy or produce it are not equally available to everyone.

G7, G8. The G7, or 'Group of Seven', consists of seven large world economic powers: Canada, France, Germany, Italy, Japan, United Kingdom, United States. The G8 also includes Russia.

GATT. General Agreement on Trade and Tariffs. Set up at Bretton Woods in 1944 at the same time as the IMF and World Bank it was a set of agreements between member countries regarding the way in which they would trade with each other. These agreements were re-negotiated a number of times. In 1995 GATT was replaced by the World Trade Organisation (WTO) which, unlike its predecessor, has power to sanction countries that don't follow its rulings.

Although GATT was not democratic, it relied on a 'consensus' process for decision making which in effect gave power to the richer and more politically powerful countries, it was more flexible and considerate of the needs of Southern countries than the WTO is and, especially in the 1970s, recognised their 'special and differential status'.

GATS. General Agreement on Trade and Services. A set of agreements the World Trade Organisation (WTO) is trying to put in place. Its aim is to control the way in which goods and services are traded across the world.

Issues

www.independence.co.uk

5

Civil rights groups complain that the powers envisaged will help multinational corporations but will undermine democracy by making national governments powerless.

GDP. Gross Domestic Product, of a nation state, the value of goods and services produced in a year, i.e. including exports but excluding imports.

GNP. Gross National Product, of a nation state, the value of all goods and services produced in a year plus income from abroad but minus income taken by foreign investors (e.g. MNCs or financial institutions).

Globalisation. Globalisation is an imprecise term, which is used to define a series of partially interlinked economic, technological, commercial, political, social and cultural processes, which have taken shape during the last decades of the 20th century. Because of the imprecision and vast scope of the notion of globalisation it is variously interpreted and remains highly contested.

IMF. A sister organisation of the World Bank and one of the Bretton Woods Trio. Headquarters: Washington. By tradition the Managing Director is European. Recent directors are: 1986-1999 Michel Camdessus (French), then Horst Köhler (German) to 2004, Rodrigo Rato (Spanish) until 2007. The current director is Dominique Strauss-Kahn from France.

The IMF was set up in 1944 to regulate the post-war global system. It is still concerned with the functioning of the world financial system but its role has changed from regulator of a managed co-operative international system to enforcer of the values and practices of a deregulated competitive open market system.

Like the World Bank, voting rights are allocated according to the size of financial contributions – rich countries pay more and get more votes.

Protectionism is the number of trading measures taken by a country in order to protect its domestic market. These could take the form of import quotas or trade tariffs

---

Interest. The price the borrower pays to the lender in return for borrowing money.

MAI. The Multilateral Agreement on Investment (MAI) was a proposed treaty aimed at giving companies greater rights when they invest overseas. Up until October 1998 it was being negotiated by industrialised countries for adoption by the Organisation for Economic Cooperation and Development (OECD), with the intention of taking the treaty on to the World Trade Organisation (WTO) and making it the international standard on investment. Negotiations on MAI stalled but more recently the same idea has emerged in the WTO under the General Agreement on Trades and Services (GATS)

MNCs. Multinational corporations (MNCs) in their most basic sense are firms that not only export their products to other countries but have also established sourcing supplies of materials, production, marketing, and managerial operations in countries other than their home base. The basic idea is not new but in recent years MNCs have become so big and powerful that authors such as Hertz (2001) argue they may be a threat to democracy.

MNCs seek to eliminate competition and typically include amongst their operations as many activities as necessary to enable them to have total control over the production and sale of their products, e.g. a clothing manufacturer will also control a packaging and shipping company. Their size and power mean they can (and do) change the location of their factories and other production units at will. If governments try to enforce environmental controls or workers try to claim higher wages or better working conditions they simply move to another country.

NAM. The Non-Aligned Movement was one of a group of organisations and programmes that came into being during the 1960s and 1970s to promote development of the Third World. It was formed by the governments of countries which had recently become independent and did not wish to align themselves with either the United States of America or the Soviet Union, the opponents in the Cold War (roughly 1945-1990).

The purpose of the NAM was to find ways to improve the position of these Third World countries in their trading relationships with their former colonial masters, the First World. Other organisations included Group of 77, Organisation of Petroleum Exporting Countries (OPEC) and the New International Economic Order (NIEO). They were inspired by Raul Prebisch's theory of 'structuralism'.

Negative resource transfers. These occur when the Third World is paying

to the industrialised countries more money in debt repayments than it is receiving in new loans and aid.

NGO. Non-governmental organisation. These are private organisations of a charitable, research or educational nature. Examples in Britain would be OXFAM and Christian Aid. There are also many NGOs in less wealthy countries. Their role is often to seek funding from abroad to provide basic welfare services.

OECD. Organisation for Economic Cooperation and Development, whose membership includes the industrialised countries of Western Europe, North America, Japan and Australasia.

Official debt. Debt owed to governments and international organisations like the IMF, the World Bank and regional banks.

Protectionism. This is the number of trading measures taken by a country in order to protect its domestic market. These could take the form of import quotas or trade tariffs.

Rate. A rate, as used in population data, is a measure of some event, or condition in relation to a unit of population, along with some specification of time. It is therefore a compound measure like speed and calculated by dividing the event or condition by the unit of population.

Birth/death rate is calculated by dividing the number of live births/deaths in a population in a year by the midyear resident population.

Infant mortality rate is calculated by dividing the number of infant deaths during a calendar year by the number of live births reported in the same year. It is expressed as the number of infant deaths per 1,000 live births.

Structural adjustment. The process by which economies change, or are forced to change, their basic structures through a reallocation of resources. Initiated principally because of balance of payments difficulties. Seen by the majority of economists in developed countries as the way to improve economic performance but criticised by many Southern economists and environmentalists and human rights campaigners globally as a main cause of the rise

in poverty the world has seen since the 1980s.

The South. During the Cold War the world was considered to be divided between those who supported the United States of America – the West – and those who supported Russia and the Soviet Union – the East. Some people in the poorer countries of the world – the countries that had been colonies of countries in Europe and had recently become independent – felt the division of the world should not be seen as East-West but rather North-South. The richer countries were in the North and the poorer in the South.

The terms 'The South' and 'Southern countries' are often used in preference to terms such as Third World.

Soviet Union – USSR. The Union of Soviet Socialist Republics (USSR) was established in 1922 and dissolved in 1991. The Soviet Union was the first state to be based on a form of Marxist socialism. Until 1989 the Communist party indirectly controlled all levels of government; the party's politburo effectively ruled the country, and its general secretary was the country's most powerful leader. Soviet industry was owned and managed by the state, and agricultural land was divided into state farms, collective farms, and small, privately held plots.

Politically the USSR was divided (from 1940 to 1991) into 15 republics: Armenia, Azerbaijan, Belorussia (Belarus), Estonia, Georgia, Kazakhstan, Kirghizia (Kyrgyzstan), Latvia, Lithuania, Moldavia (see Moldova), Russia, Tadzhikistan (Tajikistan), Turkmenistan, Ukraine, and Uzbekistan, joined in a federal union. Until the final year or so of the USSR's existence the republics had little real power. Russia, officially the Russian Soviet Federal Socialist Republic (RSFSR), was only one of the republics, but the terms 'Russia', the 'USSR', and the 'Soviet Union' were often used interchangeably.

Terms of trade. These are based on a comparison between the price of a country's imports (goods and services bought from abroad) and the price of its exports (goods and services sold to other countries).

Third World. Third World is one of many terms used to describe the poorer countries of the world. Other terms include Southern countries or the South, underdeveloped countries, less developed countries (LDCs), countries in a process of development, newly developed countries.

This term also includes a group of countries in Asia called the NICs – Newly Industrialised Countries who seemed during the 1980s and the early 1990s to be developing particularly quickly.

The wealthier, developed or industrialised countries are the First World. The Soviet Bloc was the Second World.

TNCs. Transnational Corporations – the acronyms TNC and MNC (Multinational Corporations) often get used interchangeably but TNC is gaining popularity. They are corporations that trade in many countries. The use of TNC may suggest that the author considers these companies to be so powerful as to be above the state: transnational = crossing or above nations, rather than multinational = working in many nations.

United Nations. The United Nations was formed from the former League of Nations in 1945, at about the same time as the Bretton Woods institutions. Its main aim is to persuade countries to resolve their differences without resorting to

Official debt is the debt owed to governments and international organisations like the IMF, the World Bank and regional banks

violence by establishing the norms and framework that would lead to 'the economic and social advancement of all peoples'.

The UN has a democratic structure – the General Assembly – however Assembly decisions can be over-ruled by a veto from one of the Security Council's five Permanent Members (China, France, Russia, the UK and USA). The UN is funded by its member states but it is owed over 2.5 billion US dollars, over half of which is due from the USA alone.

Most of its work is carried out by specialist bodies such as UNDP (UN Development Programme), UNICEF (children) or UNCTAD (UN Council for Trade and Development). It has debated and adopted the world's major international standards, e.g. the Universal Declaration of Human Rights and the Conventions on Women, Children, Refugees, Genocide. The UN has also sent peace-keeping forces to several countries.

Some Western nations seem happy to use the UN when it suits their foreign policy objectives but have undermined it by pulling out of crucial UN development agencies, favouring instead non-democratic bodies such as the World Bank, World Trade Organisation and IMF, in which they enjoy unchallenged power.
World Bank. A sister organisation of the IMF and one of the Bretton Woods Trio. Headquarters Washington, President since 2007 Robert Zoellick (American).

The International Bank for Reconstruction and Development (better known as the World Bank) was founded in 1944 as a means of reviving war-damaged European economies, a mandate that was later extended to developing nations. The Bank is funded by dues from members and by money borrowed in international markets. It makes loans to member nations at rates below those of commercial banks to finance development 'infrastructure' projects (power plants, roads, hydro dams) and to help countries 'adjust' their economies to globalisation. Like the IMF, the Bank was an early and enthusiastic supporter of the neo-liberal agenda.

The World Bank group also includes: the International Development Association (IDA) which makes 'soft' loans (no or very low interest) to the poorest nations; the International Finance Corporation (IFC) which tries to attract private-sector investment to Bank-approved projects; and the Multilateral Insurance Guarantee Agency (MIGA) which provides risk insurance to private investors in member countries.

Like the IMF, voting rights are allocated according to financial contributions so the countries with the largest economies have control.
World Trade Organisation (WTO). One of the Bretton Woods Trio. Headquarters; Geneva, Switzerland. Director Generals; 1999-2002; Michael Moore (New Zealand), 2002-2005 Supachai Panitchpakdi (Thailand), then Pascal Lamy (French).

The WTO replaced the General Agreement on Tariffs and Trade (GATT) in 1995. GATT was one of the original Bretton Woods initiatives which established a set of rules to govern world trade. Its aim was to reduce national trade barriers and to stop the 'beggar-thy-neighbour' actions that had hobbled trade in the pre-World War Two period. Seven rounds of tariff reductions were negotiated under the GATT treaty; the final 'Uruguay Round' began in 1986.

The WTO vastly expands the GATT's mandate in new directions. It includes the GATT agreements, which mostly focus on trade in goods. But it folds in the new General Agreement on Trade in Services (GATS) which covers areas like telecommunications, banking and transport. There are also agreements covering trade-related intellectual property rights (TRIMS) and trade-related investment measures (TRIPS). These new treaties have far-reaching implications for environmental standards, public health, cultural diversity, food safety and many other areas.

The old GATT had no legal teeth to enforce rules but the WTO can impose tough trade sanctions. The organization currently has 151 member countries.
Updated April 2008

⇨ The above information is reprinted with kind permission from De Montfort University. Visit www.dmu.ac.uk for more information.

OTHER GLOBALISATION TERMS THAT DIDN'T MAKE THE LIST...

06:46 PM

IN OUT

CAN WE AFFORD CHEESE THIS WEEK?

PAY UP

BILL

BILL

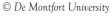

NO TOXIC DUMP

FLEXIBLE WORKFORCE

CEO EXECUTIVE SALARIES

WORKING POOR

INDUSTRY SELF-REGULATION

Concerns about globalisation

Information from the Foreign and Commonwealth Office

The following are some of the most commonly expressed concerns about globalisation.

What is globalisation's impact on inequality?

The second half of the 20th century saw unprecedented rises in prosperity throughout the world. Life expectancy in developing countries has risen from 46 years in the 1960s to 64 years today. Infant mortality rates have halved since 1960. Global sanitation coverage rose from 51% of the world's population in 1990 to 61% in 2000, which means that about 1 billion people gained access to sanitation facilities in the last decade of the 20th century.

Those countries that have grasped the opportunities offered by globalisation and have become more integrated with the world economy have reaped the greatest benefits. 'Globalising' countries, such as Chile, China, Thailand and Bangladesh, saw annual real GDP growth above 4.5% in the 1990s. In East Asia and the Pacific, where export-led growth has been strongly emphasised, the number of people living on less than $1 a day fell by 17 million between 1990 and 1998.

But, is inequality rising? In a world where the average American income is more than 100 times greater than that of a Tanzanian, first impressions may suggest it is. However, some statistical surveys show that this isn't necessarily the case and that following a peak around 1970 global income inequality has actually fallen over the past 30 years.

A common measure of inequality is the Gini Co-efficient. This looks at the way incomes are divided within a population and ranges between 0 for complete equality and 100 if a single person receives all available income. Analysis by Andrea Boltho of Oxford University and Gianni Toniolo of the University of Rome shows that the international Gini Co-efficient level fell from a figure of 53.9 in 1970 to 49.6 in 1998. A further study by Columbia University's Xavier Sala-i-Martin examines seven different popular indexes of global income inequality, all of which show growing equality between 1980 and 1998.

However, unless growth in Africa accelerates in the near future, income inequalities are projected to rise as China, India, the middle-income and rich countries diverge away from it. This is clearly a major challenge for developed and developing countries, governments and the public, who need to work together to draw the poorest into the global economy, reform international trade rules, boost investment in education and health and work to improve governance and the rule of law.

What is the impact of free trade on poverty?

Freer trade, when combined with sound domestic policies, presents enormous opportunities for economic advance in the world's poorest countries. As a recent Oxfam report argues, 'history makes a mockery of the claim that trade cannot work for the poor'.

Developing countries have a lot to gain from freer trade, through access to foreign capital, global export markets and advanced technology. It enables specialisation in areas where they have an international competitive advantage whilst delivering greater choice and lower prices to both firms and consumers.

Protectionism on the other hand raises the price of both imports and domestic products, restricting choice, and in doing so places the heaviest burden on the poorest people in developing countries. It often slows industrial change and raises its cost, inflicting damage on exporting firms by making them less competitive.

The UK government is committed to promoting equitable trade rules and an effective voice for developing countries within the international trading system. It is recognised that substantial inequities currently exist and the government will work to reduce both tariff and non-tariff barriers to developing country exports during the Doha Development round of WTO negotiations and beyond.

Do unsustainable debt burdens exacerbate poverty in the developing world?

Debt is a normal government tool, often used to finance long-term investment (in e.g. infrastructure, developing public services) and is not, of itself, bad. However, many developing countries have huge debt levels that are unsustainable, leading scarce resources needed for poverty reduction to be diverted towards interest payments to external creditors.

The UK government has been in the lead in establishing the Heavily Indebted Poor Countries (HIPC) initiative to tackle the problem of high government debt burdens in 42 of the world's poorest countries. Once a country has been deemed eligible for relief creditors then take co-ordinated action to reduce the country's external debt burden to a sustainable level.

The UK has gone further than required by our international debt-relief obligations. For the twenty-six countries who are now benefiting from debt relief, the UK is providing 100 per cent relief on all future payments to the UK. In addition, for those countries that have yet to benefit from debt relief, the UK holds debt service payments in trust for the day they can be returned to fund poverty reduction.

South East Essex College
of Arts & Technology
Luker Road, Southend-on-Sea Essex SS1 1ND
Tel:(01702) 220400 Fax:(01702) 432320 Minicom:(01702) 220642

The UK is now working hard to ensure that HIPC achieves its objective: to free eligible countries from unsustainable debt. We have been at the forefront of the international debate on the issues surrounding debt relief to ensure that HIPC delivers sustainable debt levels, which means taking a flexible and positive approach for provision of additional concessional financing and debt relief where appropriate.

What is the government doing to meet its aid commitments to the developing world?

Government spending on international development has increased markedly in recent years and will account for 0.4% of national income by 2005. This represents a 93% real-terms increase since 1997 and is a much higher level of commitment than the G7 average of 0.22%.

The government remains focused on meeting the UN target of 0.7% of national income allocated to development assistance and the extra £4.5 billion annual spending announced in July 2002 is a major step towards this. The government is pushing for others to follow our example. The proposed International Finance Facility is a potentially important complement to this, leveraging in additional money from the international capital markets to double annual development flows to $100 billion by 2015. This is the amount that experts estimate will be required every year if we are to meet the Millennium Development Goals (MDGs).

The UK has also greatly increased the effectiveness of its aid spending in recent years, particularly by making all assistance 'untied'. Aid tying is the practice of granting development assistance on condition that the beneficiary country uses the money to buy goods and services from the country granting that aid. Whilst this may initially seem like a welcome boost for British businesses it makes the assistance grossly inefficient, often leading to the provision of inappropriate goods, services and advice with costs often rising by up to 30%.

As the first major donor to fully untie, the UK's move sends a strong signal to others to reconsider their tied aid practices whilst helping to ensure that British development assistance achieves its full potential for reducing poverty.

Are the World Bank and IMF promoting inappropriate economic policies?

The World Bank and IMF work in difficult areas and the nature of the two organisations' work means that the benefits of their advice and policy recommendations may take time to become clear.

Both organisations are responding to the challenges of globalisation by becoming more open and inclusive in their decision-making and claims that they make systematic mistakes or work against the interests of the poor are misleading. The World Bank, which is owned by its 184 member countries, has poverty reduction as its primary focus. Its aim of providing vital infrastructure to the developing world is complemented by addressing issues like gender, community-driven development and the status of indigenous people. As a co-sponsor of UNAIDS the World Bank has committed more than US$1.7 billion to combating the spread of HIV/AIDS around the world.

It is also misleading to suggest that the World Bank is unaccountable and authoritarian. More than two-thirds of development projects approved by the Bank during 2002 involved the active participation of non-governmental organisations (NGOs) whilst the majority of its country strategies benefited from widespread consultations with civil society.

The portrayal of the IMF as an institution promoting inappropriate economic policies and accentuating economic upheaval is equally misguided. Countries typically only contact the organisation for assistance after all other sources of credit have been exhausted and are therefore usually in desperate fiscal straits when they approach the IMF. Providing low-interest loans, the organisation relieves, not accentuates, hardship, helping highly indebted governments limit the amount of budgetary belt-tightening required in a crisis.

The IMF is listening to its critics and seeking better ways of accomplishing its aims. However, it is incongruous to charge that misguided IMF policy advice is the main reason why debt-crisis countries face austerity.

How does globalisation affect climate change and the environment?

It is important to distinguish between globalisation and industrialisation. The latter is a process through which economies move from being largely agrarian to predominantly manufacturing and service based. Although this change is often accompanied by increases in wealth and rising living standards it has in the past usually led to increased fossil fuel use and environmental degradation.

Freer trade presents enormous opportunities for economic advance in the world's poorest countries

---

Many aspects of globalisation can be seen as good for the environment. Growing linkages between international policy makers have led to the creation of cross-border legislation for environmental protection. The Global Environment Facility and the Kyoto Protocol are two high profile examples, with the UK government committed to reducing emissions of six greenhouse gases to 1990 levels by 2010. Globalisation accelerates the development and diffusion of new technologies, many of which have led to vast improvements in the efficiency of fossil fuel use and has led to breakthroughs in the use of renewable energy sources. The spread of best practice in biodiversity conservation and the proliferation of NGOs dedicated to protection of the global environment can also be seen as aspects of globalisation.

Are transnational companies putting profits above care for the environment?

Foreign Direct Investment benefits all countries, particularly emerging markets. Foreign investors often promote enhanced social and environmental standards and practices – a process the government encourages, particularly through partnership with business to promote Corporate Social Responsibility (CSR). CSR involves private, voluntary and public sector organisations in the UK and abroad taking account of their economic, social and environmental impacts in all areas of their work.

Against this background, many businesses are actively seeking to improve their environmental performance, publishing more information about their operations and intentions on environmental issues. There is also a growing recognition that by seeking to improve environmental standards and becoming ecologically more efficient, companies can also improve their competitiveness and financial performance.

Do international companies exploit developing country workers in 'sweatshops'?

Research by the Institute for International Economics has shown that in low income countries average manufacturing wages paid by foreign companies in the mid 1990s were twice those offered by domestic firms ($3,400 per year compared to $1,700). In addition to providing jobs and higher wages firms moving to developing countries often export better working conditions and employment rights compared with those prevalent in domestic companies.

However, it is recognised that the International Labour Organisation's conventions are not always upheld. The UK has ratified all of the fundamental conventions and the government works to uphold these principles, including the abolition of forced and child labour; freedom of association and the right to organise; and non-discrimination throughout the world. In 2002/3 one of the UK's objectives was to press for more countries to ratify the ILO Convention on the Worst Forms of Child Labour. There were twenty new ratifications during this period, bringing the total number of countries to 136 by 1 April 2003.

The government also encourages the private sector to go beyond legal compliance with these core standards, and to lead on issues like improving employment conditions. We believe this action is most effective when voluntary, building on the existing framework of national and international regulation, and within a partnership between enterprises, governments and other stakeholders.

Despite the many benefits that foreign direct investment brings some sceptics argue that multinational companies should be discouraged or prohibited from operating in the developing world. This would not only deprive workers of their relatively well paid jobs but would prevent developing economies following the path of a number of countries in East Asia, where a focus on labour intensive manufacturing was a key early feature of rapid economic growth, enabling a later shift to more capital and knowledge intensive industries.

Is the power of large corporations excessive?

As the Foreign Secretary, Jack Straw, highlighted in September 2001 there is a 'widely shared concern that there is no longer any political force to check the final triumph of the multinational corporation'. Although the power of large corporations has undoubtedly grown in recent years they are far from unaccountable or uncontrollable.

Some argue that because, for example, General Motor's annual sales exceed the GDP of all sub-Saharan Africa that corporations are more powerful than countries and their citizens. This comparison is both misleading and misguided. Unlike countries, corporations do not have the power to vote in international organisations like the UN or IMF, raise revenue through taxation or imprison anyone.

Multinational companies are subject to the laws in both the countries where they are headquartered and where they operate. In addition to national initiatives and legislation, countries, companies and NGOs are working together to promote corporate responsibility through organisations such as the UN, the OECD and the EU.

Does globalisation lead to Americanisation, eroding local and national cultures?

Talking of a world of 6 billion people becoming a monoculture is

Is the world becoming a US-dominated monoculture?

misguided. Capitalism is essentially diverse, as any traveller from London to Hong Kong, Zurich or Buenos Aires will discover. Cultures are not static but are constantly evolving – any recent visitor to France will have seen that it is no less French following the introduction of the Euro.

The fact that American cultural products are successful in world markets reflects no more than their popularity and curbing global brands inevitably involves artificially restricting people's choice.

Does globalisation mean citizens and nations have lost control over the processes that affect them?

Globalisation has certainly transformed the role of the individual within the nation state and the role of the nation state both domestically and internationally. However, both citizens and governments are far from powerless and globalisation presents many new opportunities for active participation in society.

Citizens have a growing influence over the way in which corporations operate, be it as employees, shareholders or consumers. The power of consumer sentiment (in areas such as the environment and working conditions) is unprecedented and may lead to welcome improvements in companies' employment conditions or environmental impact. This consumer pressure would be much less effective without globalisation-era technology like the Internet.

⇨ Information from the Foreign and Commonwealth Office. Visit www.fco.gov.uk for more.
© Crown copyright

The Bretton Woods Institutions

Background to the issues surrounding the World Bank and the IMF

What are the Bretton Woods Institutions?

The Bretton Woods Institutions are the World Bank and the International Monetary Fund (IMF). They were set up at a meeting of 43 countries in Bretton Woods, New Hampshire, USA in July 1944. Their aims were to help rebuild the shattered postwar economy and to promote international economic cooperation.

What is the World Bank Group?

The World Bank Group is made up of five institutions, four of which were created after 1944, all sharing a similar mandate of reducing poverty and facilitating economic growth in developing countries. The original institution is the International Bank for Reconstruction and Development (IBRD), often simply known as the World Bank. Other institutions have been added: the International Development Association (IDA); the International Finance Corporation (IFC); the Multilateral Investment Guarantee Agency (MIGA); and the International Centre for the Settlement of Investment Disputes (ICSID).

How does the World Bank operate?

The World Bank is the largest public development institution in the world, lending around US$ 25 billion a year to developing countries. The main purposes of the Bank, as outlined in Article One of its Articles of Agreement, are: 'to assist in the reconstruction and development of territories of members by facilitating the investment of capital for productive purposes' and 'to promote the long-range balanced growth of international trade and the maintenance of equilibrium in balances of payments by encouraging international investment ... thereby assisting in raising the productivity, the standard of living and conditions of labour in their territories'.

Who can borrow from the World Bank?

The World Bank mainly lends to governments, although certain Bank facilities can also provide direct support to private businesses and to non-profit organisations. Middle-income countries and poorer countries termed as 'creditworthy' borrow from the IBRD, while the poorest countries borrow from the IDA. Loans granted by IDA are interest-free but borrowers are required to pay a fee of less than one percent of the loan to cover administrative costs.

How does the IMF operate?

The IMF was conceived primarily as a supervisory institution to promote international monetary cooperation and facilitate the growth of international trade. This is to be achieved through maintaining monetary exchange stability and assisting member countries who are experiencing balance of payments problems.

What types of financial assistance will the IMF provide?

The IMF provides various types of loans to member governments. Concessional loans are granted to low-income countries at a concessional interest rate through the Poverty Reduction and Growth Facility (PRGF) while non-concessional loans are provided with a market-based interest rate through five mechanisms: the Stand-By Arrangements (SBA); Extended Fund Facility (EFF); Supplemental Reserve Facility (SRF); Contingent Credit Lines (CCL); and the Compensatory Financing Facility (CCF).

What are the main concerns and criticism about the World Bank and IMF?

Criticism of the World Bank and the IMF encompasses a whole range of issues, but they generally centre around concern about the approaches adopted by the World Bank and the IMF in formulating their policies. This includes the social and economic impact these policies have on the population of countries who avail themselves of financial assistance from these two institutions.

⇨ The above information is reprinted with kind permission from the Bretton Woods Project. Visit www.brettonwoodsproject.org for more information.

© Bretton Woods Project

Globalisation – problems and solutions

Information from The Big Green Footprint

The problem

⇨ The so called 'global village' in reality means that over 1 billion people live on less than $1 a day, with the richest 20% of the world's population consuming over 80% of its resources.

⇨ Of the largest 'economies' of the world today, 51 are large multinational corporations and 49 are nation states.

⇨ Globalisation is attempting to amalgamate every local, regional and national economy into one single world industrialised system, centrally managed, pesticide intensive, monocrop production for export in order to deliver a narrow range of transportable foods to the world market.

⇨ This destruction of natural, cultural and economic diversity is leading to a massive shift of population into urban areas, which is often synonymous with slums, unemployment, poverty, pollution, crime, violence and drug abuse.

⇨ If everyone on earth consumed as much as the average person in the UK, we'd need three planets to support us – and if we consumed as much as the average American, we'd need six planets.

The root cause

⇨ Corporate power has an enormous amount of influence over Governments, enhanced by 'free trade' treaties, which allow corporations to move their operations to countries where taxes and labour costs are low and where environmental regulations are weak.

⇨ Government support for Corporations has led to a framework of subsidies that result in mass-produced goods being transported halfway around the world because they are artificially 'cheap' compared to local goods.

⇨ The root cause is a skewed approach to economics that puts profits above all else and where big businesses have little incentive to respect the rights of the communities where they operate.

> ## Of the largest 'economies' of the world today, 51 are large multinational corporations and 49 are nation states

⇨ Global bodies like the World Bank and International Monetary Fund finance major projects like dams, oil pipelines and mines that threaten local water supplies, land, homes and people's livelihoods.

The solution

⇨ Governments should create the framework where profits can be balanced with the needs of the environment and people. This means taking a more considered view that balances the long-term interests of business, government, people and the environment, rather than chasing short-term profit or vote-winning goals.

⇨ Local communities should be consulted about their transport needs, with money being put into better public transport, which would help reduce traffic, improve road safety, cut pollution and create jobs.

⇨ Friends of the Earth are campaigning for governments to agree global rules that protect the planet and give local communities priority over so-called free-trade. This means strong and binding laws that make corporations liable for their impact on communities and the environment worldwide.

⇨ One of the most successful solutions has been the growth in the local food movement – farmer's markets, box schemes etc, which is based upon the belief that locally grown food is fresher, tastier, more nutritious and contains fewer preservatives and artificial chemicals than food flown halfway around the world.

⇨ The above information is copyright to The Big Green Footprint. Visit www.thebiggreenfootprint.com for more information.

© The Big Green Footprint

51 of the largest world economies are multinational corporations

Making the global village a reality

New technology and globalisation

By Victor Keegan

Governments keep worrying about immigration and how they can prevent people from entering their countries. But while they are doing this a subtle form of exodus is taking place. People, especially early adopters, are spending more of their time conversing or doing things with people abroad, a kind of virtual migration. This is because of the explosion of social networks and a parallel phenomenon, the seemingly insatiable desire of people to spread details of their personal lives on the web to be devoured by a global audience.

At one stage it looked as though the movement might be stopped in its tracks when it was revealed that potential employers and university admission staff were combing Facebook, MySpace and other social sites to learn what candidates were really like. But there has been hardly any adverse reaction and it hasn't stopped people unburdening themselves one jot. If anything, the opposite might happen: employers are more likely to say, 'What sort of introvert have we got here who hasn't joined a social site?'

There is no sign of it stopping. Recently I have been looking at a pre-production version of Seesmic.com, brainchild of French entrepreneur Loic Le Meur, which is a kind of instant diary or blog, but using video rather than words. You record a video (dead easy now with the built-in webcams in most new laptops) then press a button and hey presto, anyone in the world can see it and respond.

The interesting point is that, unlike blogs, there is no hiding behind nicknames. This is literally in-your-face communication. It is a near-live film of you. Anonymity is strictly for the birds. Already users are making new friends across the globe and its 20,000 early testers (and 70,000 viewers a month) are becoming part-citizens of a space beyond the geography of their own country.

It reminded me that of all the new friends I have acquired in the past year (with whom I have ongoing conversations in areas of mutual interest), the majority have been in another country. I suspect this is a growing trend as a global village arrives in which people congregate on the basis of mutual interests rather than the accidental geography of where they live.

Where is all this heading? I think we can already see the parameters. A lot has already been written about Apple's new devices. They are interesting because they weren't designed by a phone company so didn't presume to provide traditional baggage such as a keyboard. For Christmas I got an iPod touch (the iPhone without the camera and phone but with a host of other functions from MP3 player to easy web-access). I am still smitten by its usability - particularly, as has been noted by others, its automatic access to the nearest Wi-Fi network. At the moment this is of limited use because - quite ludicrously - most cafes and hotels charge for Wi-Fi rather than counting it as part of the infrastructure they offer (like electricity). But that will soon change. There is an Ofcom auction later this year of spectrum suitable for WiMax that will provide fast countrywide mobile broadband at speeds of up to 20 megabytes per second, or even faster. That is four times faster than current computers at home and will be revolutionary not least in offering free phone calls anywhere in the world to other WiMax users.

Put these two things together - an iPod touch-like screen and ubiquitous broadband Wi-Fi - and suddenly everyone in the world is linked to everyone else. For nothing. You will be able to do anything from reading your paper to meeting friends from Australia in your virtual world, from the top of a 19 bus. A hint of this convergence came this week when the childrens' virtual world, gaiaonline.com, linked up with Facebook. Will we soon be spending more of our disposable time online than we do communicating with people in real life? I wouldn't bet against it.

24 January 2008

English will fragment into 'global dialects'

Traditional English is set to fragment into a multitude of dialects as it spreads around the world, a language expert claims

By Laura Clout

Professor David Crystal, one of the world's foremost experts on English, said people will effectively have to learn two varieties of the language – one spoken in their home country, and a new kind of Standard English which can be internationally understood.

The English spoken in countries with rapidly-booming economies, such as India and China, will increasingly influence this global standard, he said.

In future, users of global Standard English might replace the British English: 'I think it's going to rain', with the Indian English: 'I am thinking it's going to rain', Prof Crystal argues.

This could spell the end of the dominance of American English as the prevailing language of international affairs.

Prof Crystal said: 'In language, numbers count. There are more people speaking English in India than in the rest of the native English-speaking world.

'Even now, if you ring a call centre, often it's an Indian voice you hear at the end of the phone. As the Indian economy grows, so might the influence of Indian English.

'There, people tend to use the present continuous where we would use the present simple. For example, where we would say: "I think, I feel, I see" a speaker of Indian English might say: "I am thinking, I am feeling, I am seeing". This way of speaking could easily become sexy and part of global Standard English.'

Prof Crystal was speaking in advance of a lecture last night at the University of Winchester, on the growth and evolution of the English language.

He predicts English will become a family of languages, just as Latin did a thousand years ago.

'In much the same way as regional dialects developed, as English grows around the world it is immediately adapted to suit the local circumstances,' he said.

'There are older varieties of English such as American, South African, Australian, and emerging varieties like Nigerian, Ghanaian and Singaporean.'

However, some of the new dialects are so individual that speakers of British English would be at a loss to understand them, he said.

> **'In much the same way as regional dialects developed, as English grows around the world it is immediately adapted to suit the local circumstances'**

'In Singapore for example, "Singlish" is used on the streets but it involves so much Chinese that you and I wouldn't understand it.'

The language is in effect developing along two parallel tracks, Prof Crystal said, a phenomenon called diaglossia.

'These new dialects are expressing local attitudes which people feel very strongly about as a way of expressing who they are.

'But at the same time it is very important that there is full international intelligibility. That is fostering the development of what once upon a time we would have called Standard English – which is used in newspapers, textbooks and the like.'

The lecture was held to launch the campaign for The English Project, which hopes to be the world's first living museum dedicated to the history and evolution of the English language.

The attraction, based in Winchester, Hants, is set to open in Spring 2012, telling the story of the language from Anglo-Saxon times to the present.

Varieties of standard spoken English

Indian: He's a real enthu guy.
British: That guy is really enthusiastic.
South African: Jislaaik, china, I was in a bit of a dwaal.
British: Gosh, my friend, I was in a bit of a daze.
Australian: Bring your bathers, chuck some stubbies in the esky and we'll have a barbie this arvo.
British: Bring your swimming costume, put some beers in the cool box and we'll have a barbecue this afternoon.
Singaporean/Singlish: Dis guy Singlish damn powerful one leh.
British: This person's Singlish is very good.
Nigerian Pidgin: I no know wetin u dey yarn.
British: I don't know what you are talking about.
Islander Creole (from Colombian islands of San Andrés and Providencia): Da wan gud ting se di pikniny dem laan fi riid an rait.
British: It is a good thing that the children learn to read and write.
Cockney rhyming slang: She has such long bacons and lovely minces.
British: She has such long legs and lovely eyes.
Txt speak: 'D gr8st booty of r heritage S d en lgn, n itz r gr8st gft 2 d wrld'
British: 'The greatest treasure of our heritage is the English language, and it is our greatest gift to the world.'
5 March 2008

World trade

An overview from the National Youth Agency

What is world trade?

World trade is the trading of goods and money that takes place on an international level. When a company/person trades with another company/person from another country this is part of the world trading system. The goods we buy in the shops and the materials used to make them come from all over the world and have often been traded many times before we buy them. World trade is currently worth US$7 trillion every year.

> **World trade is the trading of goods and money that takes place on an international level**

What does world trade have to do with young people?

World trade often seems remote from young people and, indeed, from most ordinary people. In fact, we all buy these goods when they reach the shops, which means we are all intimately involved in world trade. As consumers we have the power to influence world trade for better or worse. The buying choices of young

The National Youth Agency

people in Britain affect the lives of young people on the other side of the world every single day.

Who sets the rules for world trade and makes sure they are kept?

Because world trade is international, it needs international laws. In 1995 the World Trade Organisation (WTO) was formed to govern and enforce world trade. 147 (out of 193) countries currently belong to the WTO. The governments of these countries agree to use a consensus decision making process to agree rules together, which are then enforced by the WTO. The WTO has the power to impose fines or sanctions on member countries that do not follow the rules. According to the website of the WTO: 'The World Trade Organisation (WTO) is the only global, international organisation dealing with the rules of trade between nations. At its heart are the WTO

agreements, negotiated and signed by the bulk of the world's trading nations and ratified in their parliaments. The goal is to help producers of goods and services, exporters and importers conduct their business.'

There are two other international organisations that play an indirect role in world trade. They are the International Monetary Fund (IMF) and the World Bank. Both exist to help poor countries get out of debt and the way in which they do this impacts on world trade. They have the power to give poor countries debt relief, but only if countries agree to and meet conditions, one of which is producing more food and products for international trade.

Are the rules fair?

Since 1980 the world's poorest countries have seen their share of world trade plummet by 40 per cent to less than 0.5 per cent (www.peopleandplanet.org/tradejustice). In the past five years there has been increasing concern about international trade rules and how they affect the poor and the environment. According to the Dominican Republic's Trade Ambassador: 'The WTO was supposed to have been an impartial referee of common rules ... it hasn't turned out like that. The rules are biased against the weak.'

Campaigning organisations have three main concerns:

1. Multinational companies put pressure on governments in rich countries and the WTO to agree to rules which will help them make more money. This is often at the expense of the poorest countries and the environment. This undermines the consensus decision making process which is supposed to happen.

2. The WTO believes in 'free trade', a system where there are no

barriers to trading between countries, such as import and export taxes. They claim this will help poor countries sell more goods and make more money. Opponents of free trade point out that developed countries, such as Britain and the US, became rich only by protecting their trade with the kind of taxes and rules the WTO is banning in poor countries.

World trade is currently worth US$7 trillion every year

3. The WTO often applies its rules selectively. For instance, under WTO rules governments in the developing world are not allowed to give their farmers any subsidies, as this would give them an unfair advantage over farmers in other countries. However, countries such as Britain and the US are still allowed to help their farmers with millions of pounds worth of subsidies each year. In April 2004, for the first time, a developing country (Brazil) successfully brought a case against the farming subsidies of a developed country (USA) in the courts of the WTO. This suggests that the WTO may be beginning to act more fairly in this area.

The Trade Justice Movement

In response to these concerns, a number of campaigns have begun around the world to change trade rules for the better. In Britain, more than 50 charities, NGOs and development organisations belong to a coalition campaign called the Trade Justice Movement (TJM). Between them the organisations have more than nine million supporters. The TJM campaigns for: 'fundamental change of the unjust rules and institutions governing international trade, so that trade is made to work for all. Trade justice – not free trade – with the rules weighted to benefit poor people and the environment.' (TJM website)

Fairtrade

Fairtrade is an alternative system of trade used by some food companies. It 'guarantees a better deal to producers in the developing world'. When you buy a bar of ordinary chocolate just 3 per cent of what you pay ends up in the hands of the cocoa farmer, whilst typically, more than 40 per cent goes to the company that made it and another 40 per cent to the supermarket. If chocolate has the official Fairtrade Mark on it, this is a guarantee that the farmer has received a much higher proportion of the price you pay. This is achieved partially by cutting out middlemen to buy direct from farmers, but largely by the company taking a smaller cut of the profit.

The Fairtrade Mark also means the farmer is paid in advance and has a long-term contract with the company to allow for greater security. They are paid a price that allows their families to eat properly, have access to healthcare and education and save a little money to help see them through difficult times. In other words, what every ordinary person in Britain would expect, at the very least, from their wages. The Mark is a guarantee that no forced or child labour was used to make the product. The Fairtrade Mark is given to companies in Britain by the Fairtrade Foundation, only after their chain of supply has been thoroughly inspected. Goods currently available with the Fairtrade Mark include chocolate, bananas, coffee, tea, wine, orange juice and footballs (http://www.fairtrade.org.uk/).

What is ethical trade?

The Fairtrade Mark is largely only available for food products at the moment (although recent additions include footballs and flowers). The mark may eventually be made available for clothes and other goods. In the meantime a number of small companies have strong ethical policies which, for instance, may include promising to pay workers a good price or pay them in advance or giving employment to small community groups or co-operatives in developing countries. They usually prohibit the use of child or forced labour and may also have high environmental standards. Each company has its own policy.

Although most of these companies are small, there are a few examples of national and multinational companies adopting the same kinds of policies. For instance, the Body Shop supports community trade and human rights, the Co-op Supermarket has strongly supported Fairtrade policies for many years and John Lewis is a worker's co-operative, meaning its sole shareholders are its employees.

Most supermarkets now stock Fairtrade coffee and other ethically produced products

What is the Ethical Trading Initiative?

The Ethical Trading Initiative (ETI) is an alliance of companies, non-governmental organisations (NGOs) and trade union organisations. Its goal is to ensure that the working conditions of those producing for the UK market meet or exceed international labour standards. It achieves this by asking companies to adopt their code of conduct and work towards implementing it in their chain of supply. This code prohibits, amongst other things, forced or child labour and paying below a living wage. Companies who have adopted the policy must report annually on the progress they have made. A number of high street chains belong to this initiative.

⇨ The above information is re-printed with kind permission from the National Youth Agency. Visit www.nya.org.uk for more information.
© National Youth Agency

Trade – did you know?

Information from the Department for International Development

⇨ More than 314 million Africans live on less than $1 a day – nearly twice as many as in 1981.

⇨ Removal of all cotton subsidies and import tariffs would boost global economic welfare by $283 million per year, providing a large benefit to Sub-Saharan Africa, of $147 million per year.

⇨ DFID is providing £3.22 million to Lesotho for tax reforms that have already resulted in a 204% increase in revenue collection.

⇨ In Southern Sudan DFID has provided £10 million to rehabilitate road networks to encourage links between regions and neighbouring countries.

⇨ Support to US, EU and Chinese cotton farmers is estimated to reduce world prices by 10-15%, costing farmers in West Africa $75-$100 million a year alone.

⇨ Lesotho faces 42 obstacles to trading its goods and services including poor roads and slow border crossings.

⇨ Trade in fisheries products accounts for a large proportion of the GDP of many developing countries. Fish export values are greater than combined values of tea, coffee, cocoa, bananas, rubber and sugar (FAO, 2004).

⇨ Bangladesh faces tariffs of up to 58% on its footwear exports to the US.

⇨ The generalised system of preferences (GSP) rules mean that Cambodia's garment industry cannot export clothes to the EU. Instead they face a range of EU tariffs.

⇨ Opening up telecoms services in Botswana led to a doubling of landline coverage, while the numbers using mobile phones leapt from none in 1998 to 250,000 in 2001 – around 16% of the population.

⇨ When 1 in 10 people gets access to a mobile phone in a developing country, it's estimated that national earnings rise by 0.6%.

⇨ In Mozambique an overhaul of customs management has led to a rise in tax revenue from US$86 million in 1996 to a record US$236 million in 2000 despite tax rate reductions. Imports increased by 4% in the first two years.

More than 314 million Africans live on less than $1 a day – nearly twice as many as in 1981

⇨ In Thailand, the introduction of generic competition reduced the cost of drugs for the treatment of meningitis by a factor of 14.

⇨ Asia was the poorest continent on the planet 40 years ago – twice as poor as Africa is today. It now has the fastest growing economy and is twice as rich as Africa.

⇨ The share of world exports of Sub-Saharan Africa with 689 million people, is less than one half that of Belgium, with 10 million people.

⇨ More than two-thirds of all people surviving on less than $1 a day live and work in rural areas either as small holder farmers or as agricultural labourers.

⇨ Every $1 lost through unfair agricultural trade policies costs more than $1 in rural communities because lost purchasing power means less income for investment and employment.

⇨ Over 70% of the poor in developing countries live in rural areas.

⇨ Agriculture is the largest employer in low-income countries, account-ing for about 60% of the labour force and producing about 25% of GDP.

⇨ Whole economies are being destabilised by world cotton market distortions, with poor countries bearing the brunt. Cotton exports are of marginal relevance for the United States. For Burkina Faso, by contrast, cotton represents 50% of the value of exports and is a mainstay of the national economy.

⇨ A pound of cotton can be produced for 12 pence in Burkina Faso compared with 42 pence in the US.

⇨ Rules of origin specify how much value must be added to any inputs used to produce exports that are entitled to preferences. They are often deployed as protectionist trade barriers.

⇨ A vegetable exporter in Uganda who uses imported packaging from Kenya would not be eligible for duty-free access under the EU 'Everything but Arms' scheme because of the value of the imported items.

10 September 2007

More than 314 million Africans still live on less than $1USD per day

⇨ The above information is reprinted with kind permission from the Department for International Development. Visit www.dfid.gov.uk for more information.

© Crown copyright

Trade and the WTO

The 'free trade' threat

The WTO's 'free trade' model poses a deadly threat to poor communities in developing countries. When WTO rules force these countries to open their markets to free trade, local producers are brought into direct competition with the most powerful multinational corporations in the world. The result: local firms are driven out of business, hundreds of thousands of workers lose their jobs, and millions of families are thrown into desperate poverty. Those who survive are forced into insecure or dangerous work at the margins of society.

The WTO's 'free trade' model poses a deadly threat to poor communities in developing countries.

The dangers of this 'trade liberalisation' are now widely acknowledged. Tony Blair's Commission for Africa concluded in March 2005: 'Forcing poor countries to liberalise through trade agreements is the wrong approach to achieving growth and poverty reduction in Africa, and elsewhere.' The Labour Party echoed this in its 2005 election manifesto statement: 'We do not believe poor countries should be forced to liberalise.'

Yet the Blair government has gone back on its word. The UK is working hard with its EU partners (and EU Trade Commissioner Peter Mandelson) to force open developing country markets for the benefit of big business. Government officials make no secret of the fact that this is their number one objective in the current round of WTO negotiations. Powerful industry lobby groups dictate the agenda, and the government takes it forward at the WTO.

Turning up the heat

When the current round of WTO trade talks were launched in 2001, they were dubbed the 'development round'. The WTO was supposed to put the interests of poor countries first, addressing the injustices of the current world trading system and ensuring that developing countries are able to build their own economies for the benefit of their peoples. The EU and USA would finally have to put their own houses in order (especially their unfair agricultural subsidies) and developing countries would be allowed special treatment so as to protect themselves from the threats of free trade.

The WTO's 'free trade' model poses a deadly threat to poor communities in developing countries

---

Yet once again the opposite has happened. Rich countries have wriggled out of their commitments, while poor countries have seen their proposals for special treatment rejected at the WTO. Now the EU has joined forces with the USA in the run-up to the Hong Kong Ministerial Conference, turning up the pressure on developing countries and demanding more extreme trade liberalisation than ever before.

Worse still, it is the UK that is leading the way in trying to force open the markets of developing countries. The UK government has confirmed that it is leading the charge to open up the industrial and services markets of developing countries, despite the dangers this will bring to the poor. The government says it is responding to the business agenda of British industrialists and City of London lobby groups, especially those keen to take over the banking and insurance sectors of new markets in the developing world.

Rich countries will stop at nothing to promote their business interests at the WTO. Developing countries are regularly told that they risk losing future aid packages or debt relief if they do not sign up to the trade proposals put in front of them. In some cases, individuals are threatened personally. A number of developing country delegates have lost their jobs for defending their own people's interests against the big business agenda of the rich.

Resistance

Yet developing countries are fighting back. Many have refused to bow to the pressure from rich countries at the WTO, and have made common cause to defend their interests against the increasing pressure in the run-up to Hong Kong. In this they are supported by public campaigns across the world – an international movement which rejects the WTO's damaging 'free trade' model and calls instead for the right of every people to safeguard their own future.

War on Want's partners in developing countries provide first-hand evidence of the harmful impact of free trade policies on local communities, and of the need for change. In the UK, War on Want is an active member of the Trade Justice Movement, a coalition of over 70 organisations which has campaigned for years to shift UK government policy away from the corporate agenda towards trade justice. International trade rules must work for poor people, not against them, if we really want to make poverty history.

⇨ The above information is reprinted with kind permission from War on Want. Visit www.waronwant. org. for more information.

© War on Want

Fair trade vs. free trade – which will benefit the poor?

The WTO – 10 common misunderstandings

Is it a dictatorial tool of the rich and powerful? Does it destroy jobs? Does it ignore the concerns of health, the environment and development?

Emphatically no. Criticisms of the WTO are often based on fundamental misunderstandings of the way the WTO works.

The debate will probably never end. People have different views of the pros and cons of the WTO's 'multilateral' trading system. Indeed, one of the most important reasons for having the system is to serve as a forum for countries to thrash out their differences on trade issues. Individuals can participate, not directly, but through their governments.

However, it is important for the debate to be based on a proper understanding of how the system works. This article attempts to clear up 10 common misunderstandings.

The ten misunderstandings

1 The WTO dictates policy
2 The WTO is for free trade at any cost
3 Commercial interests take priority over development ...
4 ... and over the environment
5 ... and over health and safety
6 The WTO destroys jobs, worsens poverty
7 Small countries are powerless in the WTO

WORLD TRADE ORGANIZATION

8 The WTO is the tool of powerful lobbies
9 Weaker countries are forced to join the WTO
10 The WTO is undemocratic

1. The WTO does NOT tell governments what to do

The WTO does not tell governments how to conduct their trade policies. Rather, it's a 'member-driven' organisation.

That means:
⇨ the rules of the WTO system are agreements resulting from negotiations among member governments,
⇨ the rules are ratified by members' parliaments, and
⇨ decisions taken in the WTO are virtually all made by consensus among all members.

In other words, decisions taken in the WTO are negotiated, accountable and democratic.

The only occasion when a WTO body can have a direct impact on a government's policies is when a dispute is brought to the WTO and if that leads to a ruling by the Dispute Settlement Body (which consists of all members). Normally the Dispute Settlement Body makes a ruling by adopting the findings of a panel of experts or an appeal report.

Even then, the scope of the ruling is narrow: it is simply a judgement or interpretation of whether a government has broken one of the WTO's agreements – agreements that the infringing government had itself accepted. If a government has broken a commitment it has to conform.

In all other respects, the WTO does not dictate to governments to adopt or drop certain policies.

As for the WTO Secretariat, it simply provides administrative and technical support for the WTO and its members.

In fact: it's the governments who dictate to the WTO.

2. The WTO is NOT for free trade at any cost

It's really a question of what countries are willing to bargain with each other, of give and take, request and offer.

Yes, one of the principles of the WTO system is for countries to lower their trade barriers and to allow trade to flow more freely. After all, countries benefit from the increased trade that results from lower trade barriers.

But just how low those barriers should go is something member countries bargain with each other. Their negotiating positions depend on how ready they feel they are to lower the barriers, and on what they want to obtain from other members in

return. One country's commitments become another country's rights, and vice versa.

The WTO's role is to provide the forum for negotiating liberalisation. It also provides the rules for how liberalisation can take place.

The rules written into the agreements allow barriers to be lowered gradually so that domestic producers can adjust.

The WTO does not tell governments how to conduct their trade policies. Rather, it's a 'member-driven' organisation

---

They have special provisions that take into account the situations that developing countries face. They also spell out when and how governments can protect their domestic producers, for example from imports that are considered to have unfairly low prices because of subsidies or 'dumping'. Here, the objective is fair trade.

Just as important as freer trade – perhaps more important – are other principles of the WTO system. For example: non-discrimination, and making sure the conditions for trade are stable, predictable and transparent.

3. The WTO is NOT only concerned about commercial interests. This does NOT take priority over development

The WTO agreements are full of provisions taking the interests of development into account.

Underlying the WTO's trading system is the fact that freer trade boosts economic growth and supports development. In that sense, commerce and development are good for each other.

At the same time, whether or not developing countries gain enough from the system is a subject of continuing debate in the WTO. But that does not mean to say the system offers nothing for these countries. Far from it. The agreements include many

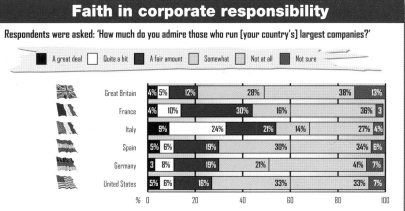

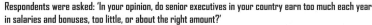

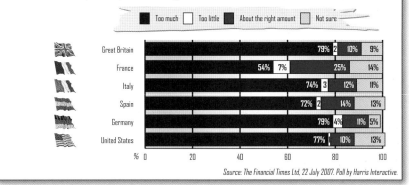

Source: The Financial Times Ltd, 22 July 2007. Poll by Harris Interactive.

important provisions that specifically take developing countries' interests into account.

Developing countries are allowed more time to apply numerous provisions of the WTO agreements. Least-developed countries receive special treatment, including exemption from many provisions.

The needs of development can also be used to justify actions that might not normally be allowed under the agreements, for example governments giving certain subsidies.

And the negotiations and other work launched at the Doha Ministerial Conference in November 2001 include numerous issues that developing countries want to pursue.

4. In the WTO, commercial interests do NOT take priority over environmental protection

Many provisions take environmental concerns specifically into account.

The preamble of the Marrakesh Agreement Establishing the World Trade Organisation includes among its objectives, optimal use of the world's resources, sustainable development and environmental protection.

This is backed up in concrete terms by a range of provisions in the WTO's rules. Among the most important are

umbrella clauses (such as Article 20 of the General Agreement on Tariffs and Trade) which allow countries to take actions to protect human, animal or plant life or health, and to conserve exhaustible natural resources.

Beyond the broad principles, specific agreements on specific subjects also take environmental concerns into account. Subsidies are permitted for environmental protection. Environmental objectives are recognised specifically in the WTO agreements dealing with product standards, food safety, intellectual property protection, etc.

In addition, the system and its rules can help countries allocate scarce resources more efficiently and less wastefully. For example, negotiations have led to reductions in industrial and agricultural subsidies, which in turn reduce wasteful over-production.

A WTO ruling on a dispute about shrimp imports and the protection of sea turtles has reinforced these principles. WTO members can, should and do take measures to protect endangered species and to protect the environment in other ways, the report says. Another ruling upheld a ban on asbestos products on the grounds that WTO agreements give priority to health and safety over trade.

What's important in the WTO's rules is that measures taken to protect the environment must not be unfair. For example, they must not discriminate. You cannot be lenient with your own producers and at the same time be strict with foreign goods and services. Nor can you discriminate between different trading partners. This point was also reinforced in the recent dispute ruling on shrimps and turtles, and an earlier one on gasoline.

Also important is the fact that it's not the WTO's job to set the international rules for environmental protection. That's the task of the environmental agencies and conventions.

An overlap does exist between environmental agreements and the WTO – on trade actions (such as sanctions or other import restrictions) taken to enforce an agreement. So far there has been no conflict between the WTO's agreements and the international environmental agreements.

5. The WTO does NOT dictate to governments on issues such as food safety, and human health and safety. Again commercial interests do NOT override

The agreements were negotiated by WTO member governments, and therefore the agreements reflect their concerns.

Key clauses in the agreements (such as GATT Art. 20) specifically allow governments to take actions to protect human, animal or plant life or health. But these actions are disciplined, for example to prevent them being used as an excuse for protecting domestic producers – protectionism in disguise.

Some of the agreements deal in greater detail with product standards, and with health and safety for food and other products made from animals and plants. The purpose is to defend governments' rights to ensure the safety of their citizens.

As an example, a WTO dispute ruling justified a ban on asbestos products on the grounds that WTO agreements do give priority to health and safety over trade.

At the same time, the agreements are also designed to prevent governments

setting regulations arbitrarily in a way that discriminates against foreign goods and services. Safety regulations must not be protectionism in disguise.

They must be based on scientific evidence or on internationally recognised standards.

Again, the WTO does not set the standards itself. In some cases other international agreements are identified in the WTO's agreements. One example is Codex Alimentarius, which sets recommended standards for food safety and comes under the UN Food and Agriculture Organisation (FAO) and World Health Organisation (WHO).

The alternative to trade – protection – is expensive because it raises costs and encourages inefficiency

---

But there is no compulsion to comply even with internationally negotiated standards such as those of Codex Alimentarius. Governments are free to set their own standards provided they are consistent in the way they try to avoid risks over the full range of products, are not arbitrary, and do not discriminate.

6. The WTO does NOT destroy jobs or widen the gap between rich and poor

The accusation is inaccurate and simplistic. Trade can be a powerful force for creating jobs and reducing poverty. Often it does just that. Sometimes adjustments are necessary to deal with job losses, and here the picture is complicated. In any case, the alternative of protectionism is not the solution. Take a closer look at the details.

The relationship between trade and employment is complex. So is the relationship between trade and equality.

Freer-flowing and more stable trade boosts economic growth. It has the potential to create jobs, it can help to reduce poverty, and frequently it does both.

The biggest beneficiary is the country that lowers its own trade barriers. The countries exporting to it also gain, but not as much. In many cases, workers in export sectors enjoy higher pay and greater job security.

However, producers and their workers who were previously protected clearly face new competition when trade barriers are lowered. Some survive by becoming more competitive. Others don't. Some adapt quickly (for example by finding new employment), others take longer.

In particular, some countries are better at making the adjustments than others. This is partly because they have more effective adjustment policies. Those without effective policies are missing an opportunity because the boost that trade gives to the economy creates the resources that help adjustments to be made more easily.

The WTO tackles these problems in a number of ways. In the WTO, liberalisation is gradual, allowing countries time to make the necessary adjustments. Provisions in the agreements also allow countries to take contingency actions against imports that are particularly damaging, but under strict disciplines.

At the same time, liberalisation under the WTO is the result of negotiations. When countries feel the necessary adjustments cannot be made, they can and do resist demands to open the relevant sections of their markets.

There are also many other factors outside the WTO's responsibility that are behind recent changes in wage levels.

Why for example is there a widening gap in developed countries between the pay of skilled and unskilled workers? According to the OECD, imports from low-wage countries account for only 10-20% of wage changes in developed countries. Much of the rest is attributable to 'skill-based technological change'. In other words, developed economies are naturally adopting more technologies that require labour with higher levels of skill.

The alternative to trade – protection – is expensive because it raises costs and encourages inefficiency. According to another OECD calculation, imposing a 30% duty on imports from developing countries would actually reduce US unskilled wages by 1% and skilled wages by 5%. Part of the damage that can be caused by protectionism is lower wages in the protectionist country.

At the same time, the focus on goods imports distorts the picture. In developed countries, 70% of economic activity is in services, where the effect of foreign competition on jobs is different – if a foreign telecommunications company sets up business in a country it may employ local people, for example.

Finally, while about 1.15 billion people are still in poverty, research, such as by the World Bank, has shown that trade liberalisation since World War II has contributed to lifting billions of people out of poverty. The research has also shown that it is untrue to say that liberalisation has increased inequality.

7. Small countries are NOT powerless in the WTO

Small countries would be weaker without the WTO. The WTO increases their bargaining power.

In recent years, developing countries have become considerably more active in WTO negotiations, submitting an unprecedented number of proposals in the agriculture talks, and working actively on the ministerial declarations and decisions issued in Doha, Qatar, in November 2001. They expressed satisfaction with the process leading to the Doha declarations. All of this bears testimony to their confidence in the system.

At the same time, the present rules are the result of multilateral negotiations (i.e. negotiations involving all members of GATT, the WTO's predecessor). The most recent completed negotiation, the Uruguay Round (1986-94), was only possible because developed countries agreed to reform trade in textiles and agriculture – both issues were important for developing countries.

In short, in the WTO trading system, everyone has to follow the same rules.

As a result, in the WTO's dispute settlement procedure, developing countries have successfully challenged some actions taken by developed countries. Without the WTO, these smaller countries would have been powerless to act against their more powerful trading partners.

8. The WTO is NOT the tool of powerful lobbies

The WTO system offers governments a means to reduce the influence of narrow vested interests.

This is a natural result of the 'rounds' type of negotiation (i.e. negotiations that encompass a broad range of sectors).

The outcome of a trade round has to be a balance of interests. Governments can find it easier to reject pressure from particular lobbying groups by arguing that it had to accept the overall package in the interests of the country as a whole.

A related misunderstanding is about the WTO's membership. The WTO is an organisation of governments.

The private sector, non-governmental organisations and other lobbying groups do not participate in WTO activities except in special events such as seminars and symposiums.

They can only exert their influence on WTO decisions through their governments.

9. Weaker countries do have a choice, they are NOT forced to join the WTO

Most countries do feel that it's better to be in the WTO system than to be outside it. That's why the list of countries negotiating membership includes both large and small trading nations.

The reasons are positive rather than negative. They lie in the WTO's key principles, such as non-discrimination and transparency. By joining the WTO, even a small country automatically enjoys the benefits that all WTO members grant to each other. And small countries have won dispute cases against rich countries – they would not have been able to do so outside the WTO.

The alternative would be to negotiate bilateral trade agreements with each trading partner. That could even include regularly negotiating the renewal of commitments to treat trading partners as equals.

For this, governments would need more resources, a serious problem for small countries. And in bilateral negotiations smaller countries are weaker.

By joining the WTO, small countries can also increase their bargaining power by forming alliances with other countries that have common interests.

10. The WTO is NOT undemocratic

Decisions in the WTO are generally by consensus. In principle, that's even more democratic than majority rule because no decision is taken until everyone agrees.

It would be wrong to suggest that every country has the same bargaining power. Nevertheless, the consensus rule means every country has a voice, and every country has to be convinced before it joins a consensus. Quite often reluctant countries are persuaded by being offered something in return.

Consensus also means every country accepts the decisions. There are no dissenters.

What is more, the WTO's trade rules, resulting from the Uruguay Round trade talks, were negotiated by member governments and ratified in members' parliaments.

⇨ The above information is reprinted with kind permission from the World Trade Organisation. Visit www.wto.org for more information.
© World Trade Organisation

Globalisation and the poor

Does globalisation benefit both developed and developing countries?

Globalisation involves the increased integration of national economies. It means a reduction in barriers of trade and investment between different economies.

The benefits of globalisation are related to the benefits of free trade

1. Consumers will have a wider choice of goods, and prices are likely to be lower. Globalisation has been an important factor in the falling price of manufactured goods.

2. Globalisation gives an opportunity for domestic firms to export to a wider market. Export-led growth has been an important factor in increasing economic welfare in Asian countries.

3. Globalisation enables increased specialisation of production. This specialisation enables firms to benefit from economies of scale. This leads to lower average costs and increased efficiency.

4. Globalisation causes increased competition between different firms and countries. This puts pressure on firms to be increasingly efficient and offer better products for consumers.

5. Increased inward investment. The process of globalisation has encouraged firms to invest in other countries. For example, many firms are relocating call centres to countries like India, where wage costs are lower. This inward investment benefits developing countries because it creates employment, growth and foreign exchange. Some foreign companies are criticised for exploiting cheap labour. But often the wages are higher than otherwise.

Problems of globalisation

1. Developing countries may struggle to compete. If a developing country wishes to develop a new manufacturing industry, it may face higher costs than advanced industries in the west, who will benefit from years of experience and economies of scale. To develop an industry it may be necessary to have protection from cheap imports; this gives the firm chance to develop and gain economies of scale.

2. Globalisation keeps developing countries producing primary products. Developing countries may have a comparative advantage in primary products, however, this offers little scope for economic growth. Primary products have a low income elasticity of demand. Therefore, with economic growth demand for products increases only slowly. Primary products often have volatile prices, this can cause the economy to be subject to fluctuations in income.

3. Multinational companies may be able to force out local retailers, leading to less choice for consumers and less cultural diversity.

4. Movement of labour. Globalisation enables workers to move easily around. However, this may cause the highest skilled workers of developing countries to leave for better paid jobs in developed countries.

⇨ Information from Economics Essays. View this piece at www.economicshelp.org/2007/05/discuss-whether-globalisation-benefits.html or visit www.economicshelp.org for more essays.

© Economics Essays

Examples of unfair trade rules

Information from the World Development Movement

⇨ **Exports:** Rich countries make it difficult for poor countries to export their products to them, by charging high tariffs and in other ways. Why should the poorest people in the world have to pay for the right to sell their wares to the richest people in the world?

⇨ **Markets:** Rich countries are pressing developing countries to open their markets to competition, and to allow uncontrolled foreign investment. But no country in the world has developed economically without protecting and supporting its own industries. All rich countries still use these tools. Double standards, or what?

⇨ **Commodities:** Big companies are making handsome profits while developing countries' economies take a battering as prices for commodities fall. Coffee is one example. Coffee farmers are now selling their coffee beans for much less than they cost to produce; but have Sainsbury's or Starbucks dropped their prices?

⇨ **Agriculture:** Rich countries subsidise their farmers. This promotes industrial, chemical-intensive agriculture that damages the environment and encourages farmers to overproduce and 'dump' their surplus in developing country markets. This is putting local farmers out of business and creating a dependence on imports to survive.

⇨ **'Patented' resources:** World trade rules allow multinational companies to 'patent' natural chemicals and products. This can lead to rapid, unsustainable exploitation of natural resources, and gives companies exclusive rights to use things which people have developed over generations.

⇨ **Natural resources:** The growing 'consumer culture' has led to unsustainable exploitation of natural resources (like metals, minerals and fuels) and production of far more waste (like plastic packaging) than the environment can handle. Trade rules and regulations on big business are urgently needed to address this and ensure global environmental and social justice.

⇨ Information from the World Development Movement. Visit www.wdm.org.uk/campaigns/trade for more.

© World Development Movement

Fighting poverty through trade

Information from the Department for International Development

Recently, the World Trade Organisation (WTO) announced a resumption of informal talks around the Doha trade negotiations. The Doha talks present the single best opportunity to promote a fair and freer global trading system, and progress in them is a top priority for both the UK and the European Union.

DFID's commitment to a successful conclusion to the Doha talks reflects its core belief that trade matters for development. Trade is a powerful engine for growth and can be an important tool for poverty reduction and meeting the Millennium Development Goals. Through Doha, and through other key channels, DFID continues to fight to make trade work for the world's poorest countries.

Doha agreement: crucial for the world's poor

The Doha Development Agenda (DDA), which sets out what the WTO talks hope to achieve, could lift millions out of poverty and integrate poorer countries into the global economy. The Agenda would create economic growth, benefiting rich and poor alike. Research (from

> **The Fairtrade movement also has a significant role to play in the fight against world poverty**

the United Nations Conference on Trade and Development [UNCTAD], the Organisation for Economic Cooperation and Development [OECD] and the World Bank) indicates that the value of this growth could be tens of billions of dollars in the agriculture and industry sectors alone. This suggests that the more ambitious the outcome of the talks, the greater the gains are likely to be.

The Doha Round commenced in 2001 with a Ministerial Conference in the Qatar capital city that gives the talks their name. DFID continues to work with other UK Government departments to ensure that the Round delivers on its original development objectives. The main strands of the negotiations relate to industrial goods, agriculture and services, and DFID wants to see developing countries' products in these areas obtain greater access to global

markets. Significant cuts in tariffs and subsidies offer the surest way for this to be achieved. Currently, low income countries exporting to the developed world face tariffs that are three to four times higher than those applied to trade between high income countries.

> **The elimination of global trade barriers could lift 300 to 500 million of the world's poor out of poverty**

DFID's development package: making trade work

In recent years, progress towards realising the objectives of the Agenda has not been as swift as originally hoped. The talks' initial deadline of 1 January 2005 passed without an agreement having been reached, and in July 2006 the negotiations were suspended because of differences of opinion between six major participating countries on the central issues of increased access to markets for agricultural and industrial products, and cuts in subsidies paid to farmers. If the barriers to trade for the developing world are to be lifted, it is essential that a deal is reached between all members in the talks. A study by the World Bank and the Institute for International Economies showed that the elimination of global trade barriers could lift 300 to 500 million of the world's poor out of poverty.

To help ensure that developing countries really benefit from new trading opportunities created by the Agenda, the UK has produced a Development Package. This takes account of the specific needs of individual countries, for example

OPPORTUNITY

safeguarding the livelihoods of West African cotton producers by reducing the support that developed countries give to their own cotton producers. The huge subsidies provided to US cotton farmers have lowered world prices by 9 to 13%, enabling the US to dominate the world market and leading to an increase in poverty in those developing countries where cotton is a major export. The Package also calls for a simplification of the complex trading rules that exempt the world's least developed countries from export duties, and a broadening of the exemptions to cover all products being exported.

Economic Partnership Agreements must help development

As well as through the DDA, another important way in which DFID is pushing to make trade address poverty is through its work on Economic Partnership Agreements (EPAs). EPAs are trading agreements between the European Union and the 78 African, Pacific and Caribbean (ACP)

countries; they are scheduled to take effect from 1 January 2008. It is vital that these agreements bring new trade and development opportunities to, and reflect the concerns of, ACP countries.

DFID is working with the European Commission and all countries involved to ensure that the agreements are development-friendly. In recent months, good progress has been made towards this, with the EU offering 100% free market access to ACP counties, with only rice and sugar being required to undergo a period of adjustment. DFID believes that trade agreements that include full access to European markets and liberal export rules will benefit poor countries and help them share in the world's wealth; over coming months, EPAs will be a priority of DFID.

In September 2007, Trade and Development Minister Gareth Thomas attended an EU Development Meeting in Madeira, where he called on the EU and ACPs to focus on the central issue of goods to achieve agreement on the EPAs by the end of the year.

A good deal for producers in poor countries

The Fairtrade movement also has a significant role to play in the fight against world poverty. By ensuring higher prices for products from the developing world, greater economic certainty, increased access to global markets, and the empowerment of producers in poor countries, the movement has already benefited some 5 million people.

Since 1997, DFID has provided nearly £2 million to the Fairtrade Foundation, and is discussing further potential support in the future. DFID wants the Foundation to focus on the poorest producers, assess impact more rigorously, expand the number of people benefiting, have an impact on mainstream supermarkets, and be able to sustain itself financially in the long term.

11 September 2007

⇨ Information from the Department for International Development. Visit www.dfid.gov.uk for more information.

'Sweatshops shame' fashion alert

British government ministers today face a warning that their failure to stop retailers exploiting overseas garment workers casts a shadow over the UK fashion industry

This warning comes from the anti-poverty charity War on Want, which attacks government inaction despite a series of scandals that have exposed British retailers profiting from clothes made by foreign garment workers on poverty pay.

The alert is signalled just before industry leaders unveil new styles in London Fashion Week, opening on Sunday (10 February).

Simon McRae, senior campaigns officer at War on Want, said: 'These scandals betray a systemic problem which shames Britain's fashion industry – garment workers in developing countries toiling long hours to produce their clothes for a few pence an hour. The industry has

failed to clean up its act. Now the UK government must legislate to stop this widespread abuse.'

War on Want lists these scandals over the last year:

January 2008
New evidence from the Garment and Textile Workers' Union in India reveals that employees producing clothes for Matalan, H & M and MK One are denied a living wage, £54 a month – enough to meet their bills for housing, food and healthcare. They receive only £38 a month – less than three-quarters of a living wage. The evidence coincides with British prime minister Gordon Brown's visit to India, where he promotes UK business at a summit with Indian premier Manmohan Singh.

December 2007
Workers are still being paid less than half a living wage producing clothes for leading UK retailers Primark,

Tesco and Asda in Bangladesh – a year after War on Want's report *Fashion Victims* exposed their sweatshops. The £4.6 million in salary and bonuses for Tesco's chief executive Sir Terry Leahy could pay the annual wages of more than 25,000 Bangladeshi garment employees who supply its stores, based on average wages of about £15 a month.

October 2007
British newspaper *The Observer* finds unpaid Indian children as young as 10 working 16 hours a day amid filthy conditions, making clothes for sale in Gap stores as Christmas gifts.

September 2007
War on Want and the anti-sweatshop coalition Labour Behind the Label name and shame 12 UK fashion stores which have cold-shouldered the only detailed study on the case for garment employees to receive a living wage. The culprits listed in *Let's Clean Up Fashion 2007 Update* are BHS, Diesel, House of Fraser, Kookai, Matalan, MK One, Moss Bros, Mothercare, Peacocks/Bon Marche, River Island, Rohan Designs and Ted Baker. War on Want and Labour Behind the Label say the culprits 'make no reasonable information available on the living wage or other labour rights issues' and 'continue not to respond to our enquiries about their policies and practice'.

British newspaper *The Guardian* reports allegations that Indian workers making clothes for British retailers Primark and Mothercare are so poor – paid as little as 13p an hour – that they sometimes have to rely on government food parcels.

August 2007
British newspaper *The Sunday Times* finds workers in Mauritius paid less than £4 a day to make clothes for the latest range designed by supermodel Kate Moss for sale by the UK retailer Topshop.

8 February 2008

⇨ The above information is reprinted with kind permission from War on Want. Visit www.waronwant. org for more information.
© *War on Want*

Sweat, fire and ethics

The sweatshop is back. Bob Jeffcott argues that citizenship is more likely to get rid of it than shopping

At the Maquila Solidarity Network, we get phone calls and emails almost every day of the week from people wanting to know where they can buy clothes that are Fairtrade-certified or sweatshop-free. Alternative retail outlets even contact us to ask whether we have a list of 'sweatfree' manufacturers. So, what are we to tell them? Unfortunately, there are no easy answers.

First, there's the cotton used to make the clothes. If you live in Canada, you may soon be able to buy a T-shirt at your local Cotton Ginny store that is both organic and Fairtrade Cotton certified. If you live in Britain, you can already purchase T-shirts and other apparel products bearing the Fairtrade Cotton label, not only through alternative fairtrade companies, but also at your local Marks & Spencer shop.

This is all to the good, isn't it? Growing organic cotton is better for the environment, and farmers are no longer exposed to dangerous chemicals. Fairtrade-certified cotton goes a step further – a better price and a social dividend to small farmers in the global South.

But what happens when cotton goes downstream? What does the Fairtrade Cotton label tell us about the working lives of the young women and men who spin the cotton into yarn in China, or those who cut the cloth and sew the T-shirt in a Bangladeshi factory before it's shipped to my local Cotton Ginny store in Toronto?

Unfortunately, very little. The Fairtrade Cotton certification is about the conditions under which the cotton was grown, not how the T-shirt was sewn.

To use the Fairtrade Cotton label, a company does have to provide evidence that factory conditions downstream from the cotton farms are being monitored by a third party; but the kind of factory audits currently being carried out by commercial social-auditing firms are notoriously unreliable. In other words, my organic, Fairtrade Cotton certified T-shirt could have been sewn in a sweatshop by a 15-year-old girl who's forced to work up to 18 hours a day for poverty wages under dangerous working conditions. So what's a consumer to do?

Well, maybe we could start by admitting the limitations of ethical shopping. Isn't it a little presumptuous of us to think that we can end sweatshop abuses by just changing our individual buying habits? After all, such abuses are endemic to the garment industry and almost as old as the rag trade itself.

The term 'sweatshop' was coined in the United States in the late 1800s to describe the harsh discipline and inhuman treatment employed by factory managers, often in subcontract facilities, to sweat as much profit from their workers' labour as was humanly possible.

Sweatshop became a household word at the beginning of the 20th century when the tragic death of over a hundred garment workers became headline news in the tabloid press across the US. On 25 March 1911, a fire broke out on the ninth floor of the Asch Building in New York City, owned by the Triangle Shirtwaist Company. Unable to escape through the narrow aisles between crowded sewing machines and down the building's only stairway, 146 young workers burned to death, suffocated, or leapt to their doom on to the pavement below. Firefighters and bystanders who tried to catch the young women and girls in safety nets were crushed against the pavement by the falling bodies.

Globalisation and free trade
In the decades that followed,

government regulation and union organising drives – particularly in the post-World War Two period – resulted in significant improvements in factory conditions. This period, in which many – but not all – garment workers in North America enjoyed stable, secure employment with relatively decent working conditions, was short-lived.

Globalisation and free trade changed all that. To lower production costs, garment companies began to outsource the manufacture of their products to subcontract factories owned by Asian manufacturers in Hong Kong, Korea and Taiwan. Companies like Nike became 'hollow manufacturers' whose only business was designing fashionable sportswear and marketing their brands. Other retailers and discount chains followed Nike's lead, outsourcing to offshore factories. Competition heightened. Asian suppliers began to shift their production to even lower-wage countries in Asia, Latin America and Africa. A race to the bottom for the lowest wages and worst working conditions went into high gear.

Today, countries like Mexico and Thailand are facing massive worker layoffs because production costs are considered too high. While most production is shifting to China and India, other poor countries like Bangladesh attract orders due to bargain-basement labour costs.

On 11 April 2005, at one o'clock in the morning, a nine-storey building that housed the Spectrum Sweater and Shahriar Fabrics factories in Savar, Dhaka, Bangladesh, collapsed, killing 64 workers, injuring dozens and leaving hundreds unemployed. Just 16 hours before the building crumbled, workers complained that there were cracks in the structure's supporting columns. Despite the lack of an adequate foundation and the apparent lack of building permits, five additional storeys had been added. To make matters worse, heavy machinery had been placed on the fourth and seventh floors.

The Spectrum factory produced clothes for a number of major European retailers, all of whose monitoring programmes failed to identify the structural and health-and-safety problems.

'Negligence was the cause of the 11 April tragedy,' said Shirin Akhter, president of the Bangladeshi women workers' organisation, Karmojibi Nari. 'This was a killing, not an accident.'

In February and March 2006 there were four more factory disasters in Bangladesh, in which an estimated 88 young women and girls were killed and more than 250 were injured. Most of the victims died in factory fires, reminiscent of the Triangle Shirtwaist fire, in which factory exits were either locked or blocked.

We need to remember that we are not just consumers: we are also citizens of the world

Twelve years ago, when we started the Maquila Solidarity Network, the word 'sweatshop' had fallen out of common usage. When we spoke to high school and university assemblies, students were shocked to learn that their favourite brand-name clothes were made by teenagers like themselves, forced to work up to 18 hours a day for poverty wages in unsafe workplaces.

Badly tarnished brands

Students who had proudly worn the Nike swoosh wrote angry letters to Nike CEO Phil Knight declaring they would never again wear clothes made in Nike sweatshops. But the big brands weren't the only villains: the clothes of lesser-known companies were often made in the same factories or under even worse conditions.

Twelve years later, the Nike swoosh and other well-known brands are badly tarnished, and the word 'sweatshop' no longer needs explaining to young consumers. Companies like Nike and Gap Inc are publishing corporate social responsibility reports, acknowledging that serious abuses of worker rights are a persistent problem throughout their global supply chain.

Today some major brands have 'company code of conduct compliance staff' who answer abuse complaints almost immediately, promising to investigate the situation and report back on what they are willing to do to

'remediate' the problems.

Yet, despite such advances, not much really changes at the workplace. On the one hand, a little less child labour, fewer forced pregnancy tests or health-and-safety violations in the larger factories used by the major brands. But, on the other hand, poverty wages, long hours of forced overtime and mass firings of workers who try to organise for better wages and conditions remain the norm throughout the industry.

Recent changes in global trade rules (the end of the import quota system) are once again speeding up the race to the bottom. The same companies pressuring suppliers to meet code-of-conduct standards are also demanding their products be made faster and cheaper, threatening to shift orders to factories in other countries. Conflicting pressures make suppliers hide abuses or subcontract to sewing workshops and homeworkers. The name of the game remains the same: more work for less pay.

Targeting the big-name brands is no longer a sufficient answer. Given how endemic sweatshop abuses are throughout the industry, selective shopping isn't the answer either.

We need to start by remembering that we are not just consumers: we are also citizens of countries and of the world. We can lobby our school boards, municipal governments and universities to adopt ethical purchasing policies that require apparel suppliers to disclose factory locations and evidence that there are serious efforts to improve conditions. We can write letters to companies when workers' rights are violated and in support of workers' efforts to organize. And we can put pressure on our governments to adopt policies and regulations that make companies accountable when they fail to address flagrant and persistent violations of workers' rights.

We should worry a little less about our shopping decisions, and a bit more about what we can do to support the young women and girls who labour behind the labels that adorn our clothes and sports shoes.

April 2007

⇨ Reprinted by kind permission of New Internationalist. www.newint.org

Globalisation and multinationals

Why the anti-globalisation mob was wrong about multinationals

By Matthew Lynn

With its £2 cups of coffee-flavoured foam and air, you might think that the one global business immune to any kind of setback was Starbucks. Over the past two decades, the company's green logo has been plastered all over the world. There have been few more successful examples of corporate branding or global expansion.

Where the anti-globalisation critics got it wrong was by arguing that big corporations are somehow 'brainwashing' or forcing consumers into buying their products

But last week saw the first real high-profile crisis since the business started to expand out of its Seattle base in 1971. With a stock price sinking faster than a double latte, it kicked out its chief executive and bought back Howard Schultz, the man who'd overseen its transformation into a global company throughout the 1980s and 1990s.

There are two interesting lessons to be drawn from Schultz's return. One is that some entrepreneurial companies often find it impossible to flourish when they don't have their key person at the helm. For example, Apple struggled until it bought back Steve Jobs. Virgin might turn out not to be up to much when it no longer has Sir Richard Branson fronting it.

The second is that the anti-globalisation mob that was so powerful at the start of this decade got its analysis of the global economy completely upside down. Starbucks, after all, was one of the main targets of its anger, portrayed as a sinister manipulative company, destroying local high streets, and forcing us all to drink bland, overpriced coffee. Others came under fire – such as Nike and McDonald's. Yet Nike has had to overhaul its strategy to pull itself out of a crisis. McDonald's has had to completely overhaul its menu.

In fact, the big brands, far from being all-powerful as their critics argued, have turned out to be intensely fragile. Far from manipulating consumers, they are constantly threatened by changing tastes, fashions and trends. That, however, isn't what we were being told a few years ago. The Battle of Seattle that accompanied the World Trade Organisation (WTO) talks in Seattle in 1999 was probably the high-point of the anti-globalisation movement. A Starbucks was the first shop window to be smashed as the riot kicked off.

Eventually, 26 of its branches had to be closed until the storm blew over. A Niketown store in the city was vandalised. And McDonald's was demonised for years.

All three companies were singled out by the high-priestess of the anti-globalisation/anti-branding movement Naomi Klein in her book *No Logo: Taking Aim At The Brand Bullies*. For a time, anti-globalisation riots were a feature of every Mayday and every meeting of the WTO or the Group of Eight. In Britain, both Starbucks and McDonald's faced local campaigns to stop them from opening up new outlets.

But since then it has become clear that Klein and her cohorts had it wrong. Starbucks now has 15,000 shops in 43 different countries and its long-term goal is to have 40,000. But its stock has tumbled by 50% in the past year, it has been forced to put out a profits warning and it has just recorded its first decline in customer numbers since embarking upon its expansion. That doesn't sound like a brand bully.

In 2005, Nike was coming under increasing pressure from rivals such as Adidas and low-cost, unbranded rivals. The response? In January 2006, the company kicked out its chief executive, William Perez, and replaced him with an internal design veteran, Mark Parker. He's pulled Nike back from crisis – but only by refocusing the company on the design of its products.

And McDonald's? The hamburger chain was subjected to a campaign for the poor quality of its food, and saw 18 months of continually declining sales and earnings in the early part of this decade. Since then, it has extensively revamped its menu, added healthier options and worked hard to improve its image.

There is nothing wrong with consumer-led campaigns. It is at least arguable that McDonald's food was cheap and nasty and not very

healthy either. Some multinationals may mistreat some of their workers in overseas factories. But consumers certainly deserve to have more information and if they don't like a company, they can make their point pretty effectively by refusing to buy the product, and convincing all their friends to do the same.

Where the anti-globalisation critics got it wrong was by arguing that big corporations are somehow 'brainwashing' or forcing consumers into buying their products. People went to Starbucks because it delivered better coffee and a better drinking environment – complete with free plug points for laptops – than the lukewarm powdered stuff and grotty décor you used to get from Joe's Café on the high street. Now the market is saturated, and there are often better competitors out there, it is running into difficulties. It is going to have to

work a lot harder to make the next 15,000 stores work – and probably start getting a lot more competitive on price as well.

Likewise, Nike and McDonald's, and many other companies that got caught up in the backlash against brands, have had to extensively reinvent themselves to stay in touch with their customers. When they don't, they suffer. Far from being sinister and manipulative, it turns out that they were at the mercy of their customers all along – which is, of course, exactly the way it should be.
16 January 2008

⇨ The above information is reprinted with kind permission from *The Business*, London's first global business magazine. Visit www.thebusiness.co.uk for more information.

© *The Business*

The fairtrade boom

7 million farming families worldwide benefit as global fairtrade sales increase by 40% and UK awareness of the Fairtrade mark rises to 57%

Fairtrade Labelling Organisations International (FLO) has announced that consumers worldwide spent £1.1bn on Fairtrade Certified Products in 2006. This is a 42% increase on the previous year directly benefiting over 7 million people – farmers, workers and their families in developing countries.

57% of adults can identify the independent Fairtrade consumer label

Meanwhile, in the UK, new figures from TNS Omnimas released today show that the Fairtrade Mark is now recognized by almost three in five British adults. The findings show that 57% of adults can identify the independent Fairtrade consumer label, up five points in just one year, and 53% of respondents correctly associated the symbol with a better

deal for producers in the developing world. UK sales of Fairtrade certified products reached an estimated retail value of £290m in 2006, an increase of 49% over the past year, and in 2007 sales are already running at an annualised rate of over £400m.

The Fairtrade Foundation is the UK member of FLO, which unites 20 national labelling initiatives across Europe, Japan, North America, Mexico and Australia/New Zealand. Global Fairtrade trade figures are unveiled to coincide with the publication of FLO's annual report for 2006/07.

Ian Bretman, Director of the Fairtrade Foundation, says: 'Britain is the second largest Fairtrade market in the world and these figures reflect the British public's appetite for Fairtrade and show great promise for the future. And consumers' increasing demand for Fairtrade products means that more farmers

are able to sell more of their produce under Fairtrade terms, strengthening their organisations, building long-term relationships and increasing benefits to their communities.'

Impressive growth figures for 2006 can be seen across global product categories, but in particular cocoa has increased by 93%, coffee by 53%, tea by 41% and bananas by 31%. Sales of Fairtrade cotton, a recent addition to the Fairtrade range, have doubled in just one year.

Sales of Fairtrade bananas grew by 31% in 2006

The growth in product sales was matched by a 29% increase from 1,514 to 1,954 in the number of licensees (companies that sell the final packaged Fairtrade products), with some companies making major commitments to supporting Fairtrade. Sainsbury's converted its entire banana range to 100% Fairtrade during 2007 and last week launched its Fair Development Fund to help make the difference in developing countries, donating £1m over four years to support producers in some of the world's poorest countries in joining Fairtrade. Marks & Spencer responded to its customers' desire for ethical products when it converted its entire tea and coffee range to Fairtrade in 2006.

Consumers worldwide spent £1.1bn on Fairtrade Certified Products in 2006

Elsewhere, global retailer and franchiser Dunkin Donuts adopted a policy of 100% Fairtrade espresso coffee in North America and Europe. Insomnia Coffee Company in Ireland converted all their coffee served from outlets across the country to 100% Fairtrade and Scandic and Hilton, one of Sweden's major hotel chains, announced that it will also switch to Fairtrade coffee.

But the Fairtrade system delivers more to farmers and workers than sales alone. Fairtrade standards ensure long-term commercial relationships between the producer and its buyer. This is absolutely fundamental in order for producers to be able to plan for their future.

Valentín Chinchay, a member of the Fairtrade certified FAPECAFES coffee cooperative in Ecuador, says: 'In 2001 and 2002, during the world coffee crises, our situation was desperate. We received between US$20-25 per quintal... many of the Ecuadorian coffee producers left. We had no choice but to abandon the coffee agriculture.' Since FAPECAFES became Fairtrade Certified in 2003, the difference that

Fairtrade made has been remarkable. 'We are currently selling 80% of our total coffee production under Fairtrade terms. For our Fairtrade organic coffee we are receiving US$139 per quintal and US$119 per quintal for our conventional Fairtrade coffee. But more important than the higher prices is the stability that Fairtrade brings. We are not as vulnerable to market volatility as we used to be,' says Valentín. During 2006, FLO estimates that Fairtrade coffee sales provided an estimated €41m more to Fairtrade certified Coffee Cooperatives than selling their products under conventional terms.

But despite growing by on average 40% per year over the last five years, the Fairtrade market still has plenty of room for expansion. In fact, FLO estimates that just 20% of the total production of Fairtrade certified producers is sold under Fairtrade terms. FLO and its member Labelling Initiatives are working to open new markets and identify new business opportunities for producers so that Fairtrade certified producer organisations can increase the percentage of their production sold under Fairtrade terms in the future.

Ian Bretman adds: 'While recognising the contribution Fairtrade has made to farming families over the last 10 years, we cannot be satisfied. Too many producers all over the world continue to suffer from unfair trade, often struggling to cover the cost of production. Similarly, too many workers in developing countries endure low wages, poor working conditions and are often denied the freedom to join a union. Besides continuing to lobby governments to make changes on international trade rules in favour of the poorest countries, incorporating Fairtrade products in our daily shopping routine is a way to send a powerful message to industry and eventually force companies and governments to rethink their business models and policies. We need people to shout even louder, and we need companies to respond with genuine engagement so that millions of farmers will be lifted out of poverty. The millions of people who are choosing Fairtrade when they go shopping are making this happen and we hope the upward trend will continue.'
10 August 2007

⇨ The above information is reprinted with kind permission from the Fairtrade Foundation. Visit www.fairtrade.org.uk/schools for more information.

© *Fairtrade Foundation*

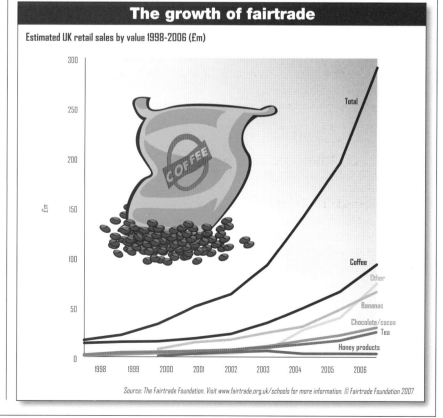

The growth of fairtrade

Estimated UK retail sales by value 1998-2006 (£m)

Source: The Fairtrade Foundation. Visit www.fairtrade.org.uk/schools for more information. © Fairtrade Foundation 2007

'Teach us how to fish – do not just give us the fish'

Does buying Fairtrade products really make a difference to people's lives? Rachel Dixon talks to three producers and finds out how their communities have been transformed

Gerardo Arias Camacho, coffee producer, Costa Rica

Gerardo is a coffee farmer in Llano Bonito, San José, Costa Rica. He is a board member on his village cooperative, which is a member of the Fairtrade consortium COOCAFE. He is married with three children.

In the 1980s, the price of coffee fell so low that it didn't cover the cost of production. Many farmers abandoned their land and went to the cities to find work. Some even left the country. In the mid-90s, I decided to go to America to make money and support my family. After eight years, I had earned enough to buy the family farm so that my parents could retire. But coffee prices were still so low that I was forced to go back to the States for another two years.

The coffee market was so unstable. We did not have a local school, good roads or bridges. Now that our consortium is Fairtrade-certified, prices are stable and we receive a guaranteed premium. We spend the money on education, environmental protection, roads and bridges, and improving the old processing plant. We have sponsored a scholarship programme so that our kids can stay in school.

I believe that my cooperative would be out of business if it wasn't for Fairtrade. Free trade is not responsible trade. When prices go down, farmers produce more and prices drop further. Fairtrade is the way trade should be: fair, responsible and sustainable.

My oldest son is in college, my ten-year-old has already had as much education as me, and my little princess is in her second year at school. With the help of Fairtrade, they might all be able to go to university and get a degree. They won't have to jump the border from Mexico to America,

leaving their country for ten years, like me. They can decide what they want in life. I tell them: 'You have two choices. You can be a coffee grower or you can be something else. But learn how to be a coffee grower first, like your father and your grandfather.'

Since Fairtrade, our farms have become more environmentally friendly. Our coffee is now produced in a sustainable way. We have planted trees and reduced the use of pesticides by 80% in 10 years. We used to cut 20 hectares (50 acres) of forest down every year to fuel the ovens at our processing plant. Now we have a new oven which is fuelled by waste products, including coffee skins and the skins of macadamia nuts that we buy from farmers on the other side of Costa Rica. It is a win-win business.

Fairtrade is not a closed system, it is open to everyone. But we need more and more people to buy Fairtrade so that the market grows and other farmers can become certified. Fairtrade can be a tool to help farmers who are not certified. We educate the producers around us about market prices so that buyers have to offer them a competitive rate. It also benefits the wider community. When there was a hurricane, the new road became blocked and the bridge

came down. We could afford to open the road and fix the bridge.

When you are shopping, look for the Fairtrade label – you can be sure that the money is going straight to the producers. It will help us, but it will also help people around the world, because the benefits of protecting the environment are for everyone. It is a matter of helping each other.

As a Fairtrade farmer, I finally feel competitive – I feel that I have a tool in my hand. It has given me knowledge, so that I am more able to defend myself and my people. I feel there is a future in front of us, because we can stay in our own country and make a living growing coffee.

Fairtrade is not charity. Just by going shopping, you can make a difference.

Julius Ethang'atha, tea producer, Kenya

Julius is a retired tea producer from Michimikuru, Kenya. He helped to introduce Fairtrade tea production to Kenya five years ago, while working for the Kenya Tea Development Agency (KTDA).

You can't keep all your eggs in the same basket, so we try many things in Kenya. I tried tea. When I was working for the KTDA, buyers asked for Fairtrade. It wasn't easy to become certified, but I saw it was the best way out for our people.

There was a huge impact on the first communities to work with Fairtrade. They were poor communities; they did not have water, dispensaries or schools close to them. The money they got from tea was used for food and clothes, but now they also get a premium that they can use to improve their social living. So far they have set up impressive schools and daycare centres, dispensaries, maternity units, water systems, bridges and roads.

I think criticism of Fairtrade is ridiculous. Yes, Fairtrade only accounts for a small share of the cake, but it is growing. Saying 'Do not buy Fairtrade, because it doesn't help non-Fairtrade producers' is like saying 'Do not eat, because others are hungry'.

Africa does not need aid; we need to participate in a fairer trading system. Teach us how to fish – do not just give us the fish. You see, the farmer receives just 5% of the wealth in tea. When the consumer pays more for Fairtrade tea, this extra money goes to the farmer and improves lives. But if the whole value chain was made fairer, Africa would be lifted out of poverty.

Fairtrade is the right way to shop. It puts a smile on the faces of children in Africa, and it makes their lives bearable.

Makandianfing Keita, cotton farmer, Mali

Makandianfing is a cotton farmer in Dougourakoroni village, Mali, west Africa. The village cotton farmers are members of the UC-CPC de Djidian cooperative, which has been Fairtrade-certified since 2005. Makandianfing married last year.

Cotton prices were going down and down until they were below the cost of production. People were demotivated and it was very depressing. But now, we can make a sustainable living. My family can eat and we have better health.

In the past, children had to walk 10km to go to school, so really it was impossible. We have now been able to build a school. At first it had two classrooms. When we had more money and wanted to expand, we challenged the government to match our investment. Now there are five classrooms in total, and every child in the village can go to school.

Pregnant women had no access to healthcare. Many died in childbirth and there were high rates of infant mortality. Now we have built a maternity centre. We have also built a food storage facility so that we can have a year-round food supply, and we have installed a pump for drinking water. We have built a new road, enabling us to travel further than 5km outside of the village without difficulty.

Fairtrade standards called for better agricultural practices. Before, empty pesticide containers would be used as water carriers. In some cases this led to death. Now, we dispose of waste properly. We don't burn bushes any more, we prevent soil erosion and we have effective irrigation.

Fairtrade has really changed the life of my community. I feel as though I have a future, which I didn't before. My wife is pregnant with our first child – this is how optimistic we are!

I encourage everyone to buy more Fairtrade products if they want to make an impact on millions of lives.
12 March 2008

© *Guardian Newspapers Limited 2008*

Unfair trade?

Adam Smith Institute: fair trade is unfair, says think-tank

According to the Adam Smith Institute's latest report, *Unfair Trade* by Marc Sidwell, Fairtrade Fortnight is little more than a marketing exercise intended to maintain Fairtrade's predominance in an increasingly competitive marketplace for ethically-branded products. The hype is necessary, because there is every reason for the shrewd consumer to make other choices.

The report highlights the inconvenient truths about 'Fair' trade:

⇨ Fair trade is unfair. It offers only a very small number of farmers a higher, fixed price for their goods. These higher prices come at the expense of the great majority of farmers, who – unable to qualify for Fairtrade certification – are left even worse off.

⇨ Many of the farmers helped by Fairtrade are in Mexico, a relatively developed country. Few are in places like Ethiopia, as people commonly assume.

⇨ Fair trade does not aid economic development. It keeps the poor in their place, sustaining uncompetitive farmers on their land and holding back diversification, mechanisation, and moves up the value chain. This denies future generations the chance of a better life.

⇨ Fair trade helps landowners, rather than the agricultural labourers who suffer the severest poverty. Fairtrade rules actually make it harder for labourers to gain permanent, full-time employment.

⇨ Just 10% of the premium consumers pay for Fairtrade actually goes to the producer. People further along the retail chain take the rest.

⇨ Four-fifths of the produce sold by Fairtrade-certified farmers ends up in non-Fairtrade goods. At the same time, it is possible that many goods sold as Fairtrade might not actually be Fairtrade at all.

⇨ The consumer now has a wide variety of ethical alternatives to Fairtrade, many of which represent more effective ways to fight poverty, increase the poor's standard of living and aid economic development.

As the ASI's policy director, Tom Clougherty, says:

'At best, fair trade is a marketing device that does the poor little good. At worst, it may inadvertently be harming some of the planet's most vulnerable people. If we really want to aid international development we should instead work to abolish barriers to trade in the rich world, and help the developing world to do the same. Free trade is the most effective poverty reduction strategy the world has ever seen.'

You can download the report as a PDF here: http://www.adamsmith. org/images/pdf/unfair_trade.pdf
25 February 2008

⇨ The above information is reprinted with kind permission from the Adam Smith Institute. Visit www.adamsmith.org for more information.

© *politics.co.uk*

Globalisation will not threaten skilled UK workers

National Outsourcing Association claims globalisation is no threat to highly skilled UK jobs

The National Outsourcing Association (NOA) has hit back at MP claims that globalisation will threaten highly skilled jobs in the UK.

It follows a report published earlier this week by the Treasury Select Committee, which warns that 'an inexorable shift in global economic power from West to East is under way', with China, India and Brazil set to become economic 'powerhouses'.

> **'We believe that globalisation will help rather than hinder the UK economy. The growth of the global market will boost the UK economy, and lead to job creation across the board'**

MPs urged for action to be taken to minimise the impact of globalisation on high and low-skilled workers within the UK. They added that some jobs within the low-skilled service sector could not be done by cheap overseas labour.

However, the NOA said: 'We disagree – we believe that globalisation will help rather than hinder the UK economy. The growth of the global market will boost the UK economy, and lead to job creation across the board.'

According to the outsourcing body, the continuous demand for cheap products and services and global competition drove up high labour-intensive processes towards low labour cost areas, whether skilled or unskilled.

'This isn't the fault of outsourcing any more than workers in earlier times striking against machines taking their jobs is the fault of the machines,' it said. 'This is a by-product of globalisation, but not necessarily one that will have negative consequences.'

The NOA challenged the local economy to react to an increase in low labour cost areas, by developing the skills and competencies necessary to develop new products, designs and technologies, so as to create better value. 'This means better education, training, entrepreneurship and supporting the cultural side,' it said.

'At the highest end [management and director level within companies], there is already a highly educated and trained workforce, so the human capital for professional jobs is already there. It is at the lower, less skilled end of the spectrum where both outsourcing and globalisation have been more widely accused of shipping jobs,' the NOA concluded.

19 October 2007

⇨ The above information is reprinted with kind permission from Personnel Today. Visit www.personneltoday. com for more information.

© Personnel Today

Some companies have already chosen to move services such as call centres outside the UK

Offshoring and UK workers

UK population feels increasingly threatened by offshoring with 82% not wanting more jobs moving overseas. 65% believe more investment is needed in skills and education for the UK to maintain current competitive economic position

The UK public perceive offshoring to be an increasing threat with 82% believing enough jobs have moved offshore already, according to a Deloitte/YouGov survey of attitudes to global economic competition published to coincide with the 2006 CBI annual conference. Just 4% of respondents support the continuation of offshoring and almost 1 in 3 (32%) believe UK companies should be forced to bring jobs back to the UK.

Public attitudes towards offshoring have become more negative since the survey was initially conducted in January this year when 22% of respondents thought UK companies should be forced to bring jobs back to the UK. In January 29% said they could see the advantages of offshoring, or even thought it was a good thing, compared with just 13% now. Several announcements have been made in the past 10 months on plans to increase offshoring across a variety of sectors.

David Owen, consulting partner at Deloitte, comments: 'There are clearly personal concerns over job security behind the negative attitudes to offshoring and our own insights suggest we can expect massive increase in the financial services sector alone. Growing awareness of the increased mobility of both resource and labour is causing anxiety with 17% of respondents believing that offshoring presents a threat to their own jobs while a further 25% think the increasing number of workers migrating to the UK is their biggest threat.'

When asked which countries posed the biggest challenges to the UK economy over the next five years, the emerging economies of China (76%) and India (48%) came out top, followed by the US (34%) and Japan (32%). David Owen commented: 'The speed and energy with which India and China are increasingly

competing on equal footing was a key subject of debate at the CBI conference this week and the fact is that these economies have the potential to create major openings for UK companies.

'As the world's leading recipient of inward Foreign Direct Investment, the UK is experiencing a huge in-flow of companies from India and China, with a surge of listings over the past three years on both LSE and AIM. Companies are investing in the UK because of its open-door policy and the nexus of business and financial services around London – which now offers the best breadth and depth of professional services skills sets and depth of international perspectives in the world. This is not to say the UK is without challenges, we still need to ensure that we are competitive from a tax and regulation perspective.'

65% of survey respondents said that investment in education and training was required for the UK to maintain global competitiveness (75% in January); the next highest being more encouragement for small business start-ups and entrepreneurialism 57% (69% in January). When asked which sectors the UK was most likely to be a world leader in, financial services came out top (32%), followed by professional services (25%), media and creativity (26%) and telecommunications and technology combined at 24%.

John Kerr, managing partner for innovation at Deloitte, comments:

'The transfer of jobs at some skill levels is a trend that is likely to continue and brings with it opportunities as well as threats. The UK needs to be in a position to benefit from operations moving offshore, rather than be threatened by the increasingly global nature of the product and services markets and this is front of mind with our top business leaders. In the financial services sector, for

example, there is a huge amount of reinvestment of the cost saving made through offshoring to develop the high value end of the business and this should encourage the UK public to feel more optimistic.

'If the UK is to thrive as a world leader in financial and professional services and media and technology sectors as the public predicts, then we clearly need a highly skilled workforce to fill these roles and this is recognised

Other key findings

⇨ 50% of respondents believe that the UK status as a global power is declining while 5% think it is increasing.

⇨ 69% of respondents believe that Government is responsible for global competition (down from 77%).

⇨ 38% of respondents believe that business is responsible for global competition (down from 52%).

⇨ 66% of those questioned said they would relocate internationally to be better off financially.

⇨ 64% said they would move to improve their work/life balance.

⇨ 53% would leave the UK for better education and skills training.

This time last year a separate Deloitte report, *Trading Places*, ranked the UK as sixth most competitive place to do business, amongst 25 major world economies. However, this ranking was projected to slide to 12th place within the next five years if UK Government and businesses do not work together to ensure the macroeconomic environment, skills, investment, enterprise and innovation continues to be world class in the UK.

by the public in the call for more investment in education and training. We hear frequent warnings of future skill gaps in many of these sectors and this brings urgency to the need for the UK to identify the key areas of potential weakness for the UK and to take actions on issues such as learning and skills, training, regulation and their link with productivity.'
28 November 2006

Britain and globalisation: a good marriage

The benefits of globalisation for Britain will survive the social unease caused by immigration and ethnic diversity, says Merril Stevenson

The news out of Birmingham, England's second city, this week is grim indeed. If reports of an alleged plot to kidnap and kill a British Muslim soldier, broadcasting the events by internet, turn out to be well-founded, it marks a relatively new and certainly gruesome development. Importing terrorist tactics from Baghdad to Birmingham is, I suppose, a dark form of 'globalisation'. It is certainly helping to give the other, economic, sort – the increasing mobility of capital, goods and services, and labour – a bad name.

But don't knock globalisation, for Britain owes much of its current prosperity to it – as I have explored in a report for the *Economist* ('Britannia redux', 2 February 2007). A quarter-century ago, few would have expected British GDP per head to be higher today than Germany's or France's, but so it is: Britain has enjoyed the longest stretch of steady economic growth since the early 1970s. Employment is at record levels and inflation has for the most part been well-behaved. And with prosperity has come renewed global clout: Britain has helped to shape European enlargement, aid to Africa, the debate on climate change and, most recently, negotiations to restart world-trade talks.

Britain got its economic act together just as globalisation was accelerating, in the late 1980s. It has managed to catch and ride the current wave successfully, selling the world financial and business services where once it sold cotton textiles and machines. Shifting earlier and more decisively than most countries out of mass manufacturing, where it had few advantages over lower-cost competitors, to more easily defended high-value-added goods and services gave it an edge. Margaret Thatcher's painful union-bashing left Britain with flexible labour markets at a time when countries such as France and Germany are struggling with unbudgeable workers and high unemployment. Strengthening competition – blowing open the City in the 'big bang' of 1986, letting in foreign investors with new ideas – has also sharpened everyone's game.

Spots on the sun

Britons as a whole are better off with globalisation: consumer goods cost less, and so do mortgages, for example. But there are painful and wrenching changes afoot as well which harm individuals. Three areas that pose tough questions for globalisers are jobs, corporate control and immigration.

First, some 2.5 million extra jobs have been created since Labour came to power, but over 1m manufacturing jobs have been lost too. A lot of the jobs that have gone were more secure and better paid than the new ones, and not all the people made redundant were able to secure even hamburger-flipping employment. And it's not only manufacturing jobs that have gone: so have many from

call-centres and data-processing, for example, and fancier jobs too are beginning to migrate.

Some of this is globalisation's fault but more of it is probably technology's. It is now possible to answer phones and design warehouses and analyse company accounts at a distance and transmit the results instantly, so it is logical to do those things where the cost/quality ratio is best. The answer is surely not to keep people in jobs in which they are not competitive but to make sure they are equipped to get new, better ones. That is where attention should be focused.

A second neuralgic issue is the flood of takeovers of British companies by foreign firms. The steel group Corus, it seems, is to go to India's Tata; and the courtship of the London Stock Exchange by Nasdaq, an American electronic exchange, has long since turned into a siege. Britons are more accustomed to being the acquirers, and this role reversal is unwelcome to many.

Foreign corporate control does raise concerns. Some fear the 'headquarters effect': that a foreign owner is more likely to close a foreign plant than one at home or to choose an auditor down the road from head office. Others worry, especially recently, that a number of deals are designed merely to milk quasi-monopolies or strip

assets. Britain is particularly open to inward investment, and British firms are not always able to buy abroad with equal ease.

But much foreign investment brings specific benefits – capital, new management or production techniques, employment. A number of studies suggest that productivity is higher in multinational firms in Britain than in most domestic ones. A competitive market in corporate control brings a more general benefit too: by threatening company bosses with takeover it makes them compete harder to stay in business. It is difficult to say where ownership lies anyway when investors buy shares the world over. Other countries may want to shoot themselves in the foot by keeping out foreign investment but that is no reason why Britain should.

Immigration is a third issue where globalisation helps more than it hurts, but does some of both. The flow of foreigners into Britain has increased over the past ten years, partly because a growing economy has demanded more workers and partly because disruption elsewhere – plus European enlargement – has boosted supply. Immigrants have undoubtedly kept wages down and most likely taken some jobs from those that wanted them. But they have also lifted economic output and contributed

needed skills. The choice does not always come down to outsourcing work abroad or importing people to do it; but when it does, surely Britain benefits more by importing the labour and the knock-on economic activity it generates.

These arguments pale, however, next to the social unease that immigration and ethnic diversity are causing, especially now that Islamist terrorism has reared its head. A debate – indeed a definition – of multiculturalism awaits another blog. What matters is that the benefits of globalisation, which has done much for Britain now and in the past, not be thrown out in reaction to the latest report of clear and present danger. Britons have supported freer trade since before the repeal of the Corn Laws. They should not abandon it now.

Merril Stevenson is the Britain editor of the *Economist*, and author of its report 'Britannia redux', published on 1 February 2007.

2 February 2007

⇨ This article was originally published in the independent online magazine www.opendemocracy.net as part of a debate 'Britannia redux?' published in conjunction with the *Economist*. You can visit the debate at http://www.opendemocracy.net/globalization-britannia_redux/debate.jsp

© *Open Democracy*

Making globalisation work

Economic globalisation has outpaced the globalisation of politics and mindsets. It's time for change

I have written repeatedly about the problems of globalisation: an unfair global trade regime that impedes development; an unstable global financial system that results in recurrent crises, with poor countries repeatedly finding themselves burdened with unsustainable debt; and a global intellectual property regime that denies access to affordable life-saving drugs, even as Aids ravages the developing world.

I have also written about globalisation's anomalies: money should flow from rich to poor countries, but in recent years it has been going in the

By Joseph Stiglitz

opposite direction. While the rich are better able to bear the risks of currency and interest-rate fluctuations, it is the poor who bear the brunt of this volatility.

Indeed, I have complained so loudly and vociferously about the problems of globalisation that many have wrongly concluded that I belong to the anti-globalisation movement. But I believe that globalisation has enormous potential – as long as it is properly managed.

Some 70 years ago, during the Great Depression, John Maynard Keynes formulated his theory of unemployment, which described how government action could help restore full employment. While conservatives vilified him, Keynes actually did more to save the capitalist system than all the pro-market financiers put together. Had the conservatives been followed, the Great Depression would have been even worse and the demand for an alternative to capitalism would have grown stronger.

By the same token, unless we recognise and address the problems of globalisation, it will be difficult to sustain. Globalisation is not inevitable: there have been setbacks before, and there can be setbacks again.

Globalisation's advocates are right that it has the potential to raise everyone's living standards. But it has not done that. The questions posed by young French workers, who wonder how globalisation will make them better off if it means accepting lower wages and weaker job protection, can no longer be ignored. Nor can such questions be answered with the wistful hope that everyone will someday benefit. As Keynes pointed out, in the long run, we are all dead.

Growing inequality in the advanced industrial countries was a long-predicted but seldom advertised consequence of globalisation. Full economic integration implies the equalisation of unskilled wages everywhere in the world, and, though we are nowhere near attaining this 'goal', the downward pressure on those at the bottom is evident.

To the extent that changes in technology have contributed to the near stagnation of real wages for low-skilled workers in the United States and elsewhere for the past three decades, there is little that citizens can do. But they can do something about globalisation.

Economic theory does not say that everyone will win from globalisation, but only that the net gains will be positive, and that the winners can therefore compensate the losers and still come out ahead. But conservatives have argued that in order to remain competitive in a global world, taxes must be cut and the welfare state

reduced. This has been done in the US, where taxes have become less progressive, with tax cuts given to the winners – those who benefit from both globalisation and technological changes. As a result, the US and others following its example are becoming rich countries with poor people.

Globalisation's advocates are right that it has the potential to raise everyone's living standards. But it has not done that

---

But the Scandinavian countries have shown that there is another way. Of course, government, like the private sector, must strive for efficiency. But investments in education and research, together with a strong social safety net, can lead to a more productive and competitive economy, with more security and higher living standards for all. A strong safety net and an economy close to full employment provides a conducive environment for all stakeholders – workers, investors, and entrepreneurs – to engage in the risk-taking that new investments and firms require.

The problem is that economic globalisation has outpaced the globalisation of politics and mindsets. We have become more interdependent, increasing the need to act together, but we do not have the institutional frameworks for doing this effectively and democratically.

Never has the need for international organisations like the

IMF, the World Bank, and the World Trade Organisation been greater, and seldom has confidence in these institutions been lower. The world's lone superpower, the US, has demonstrated its disdain for supranational institutions and worked assiduously to undermine them. The looming failure of the Development Round of trade talks and the long delay in the United Nations Security Council's demand for a ceasefire in Lebanon are but the latest examples of America's contempt for multilateral initiatives.

Enhancing our understanding of globalisation's problems will help us to formulate remedies – some small, some large – aimed at both providing symptomatic relief and addressing the underlying causes. There is a broad array of policies that can benefit people in both developing and developed countries, thereby providing globalisation with the popular legitimacy that it currently lacks.

In other words, globalisation can be changed; indeed, it is clear that it will be changed. The question is whether change will be forced upon us by a crisis or result from careful, democratic deliberation and debate. Crisis-driven change risks producing a backlash against globalisation, or a haphazard reshaping of it, thus merely setting the stage for more problems later on. By contrast, taking control of the process holds out the possibility of remaking globalisation, so that it at last lives up to its potential and its promise: higher living standards for everyone in the world.

Published in the Guardian, *7 September 2006*

© *Project Syndicate/Institute for Human Sciences*

THE GLOBALISED FREE MARKET ECONOMY PREMISE:

RAISED LIVING STANDARDS

GLOBAL TRADE LEVEL PLAYING FIELD

CONSUMER POWER (MORE CHOICE!)

COMPLETE EFFICIENCY

CHEAP IMPORTS - LOSS OF LOCAL MANUFACTURE INDUSTRIES

LOWER WORKERS' WAGES - HIGHER EXECUTIVE SALARIES

UNREALISTIC MARKET GROWTH

LOSS OF INDIVIDUAL LIBERTIES

UNDERMINING OF THE WELFARE STATE

INCREASED POWER OF CORPORATIONS

UNSUSTAINABLE LIFESTYLE

THE REALITY... FOR MANY

Attitudes to global trade

Global @dvisor survey reveals sharply contrasting attitudes – the world's most engaged consumer-citizens embrace global trade and investment, but want their governments to increase regulation on companies

The world's most engaged citizens say that while they personally embrace global trade and corporate investment in their homeland, they want their governments to more aggressively crack down on the activities and influence of national and multinational corporations, a new survey reports today.

The survey by leading research firm Ipsos, covering a new breed of influencers in 20 of the world's leading and burgeoning powerhouse economies, highlights the risk for global and national corporations because potential government intervention and tighter regulatory regimes will be backed by their most engaged citizens.

Encompassing 20,000 interviews, the survey shows a large majority (71%) of these socio-political activists feeling that foreign companies have too much influence over the economy in their country, and even more (75%) believing their government should be more aggressive in regulating corporations.

Comments Stewart Lewis, Head of the Ipsos MORI Reputation Centre:

'Our survey illustrates the importance of a new breed of social and political activists (SPAs) that have grown up around the world. These influencers are engaged citizens who lead and stir debate. They galvanise public opinion by directly and indirectly pressurising business and government. They are consumer-oriented and drive others to reward and punish good and bad corporate behaviour. As a result they are a force to be reckoned with; industry and governments ignore these individuals at their peril.'

Despite their desire for greater regulation of companies within their countries, these engaged individuals are actually global trade and corporate investor supporters, not the expected stereotype.

Among other findings, 91% believe that expanding global trade is a 'good' thing, another 81% advocate that investment by global companies in their country is essential for their growth and expansion, and two-thirds (63%) agree that overall, globalisation is a good thing for the world.

The survey audience represents an intelligent, active and engaged population. Half have instigated political, social and economic discussions, and 37% have signed a petition in the past year. All are online; half are under 35; half have university-level education. They translate their concerns into their behaviour as consumers, and lead by example. Almost half (47%) have chosen to buy a product or service on the basis of the company's ethical, social or environmental reputation, while a third (33%) have advised others against buying from a specific company on the same grounds.

The 20-country Ipsos survey shows that China and India are by far the most optimistic about their future; these optimists outweigh the pessimists by 41%; Russia is some way behind in third place. In most of the developed countries, pessimists outnumber optimists – including the US, Germany and especially Britain.

However, the stereotypical view that developing countries focus on material improvement while the developed world cares more about social and environmental issues is well wide of the mark. According to this survey it is developing countries that call for increased regulation, with environmental protection at the top of their agenda.

SPAs are more positive than negative about the influence of the military, major corporations, the World Bank, the media and their political leader on their country. The opposite is true of their attitudes

towards national governments, justice systems, unions, religious leaders and pressure groups. Most countries see the influence of the military on their country as a positive, especially India; the exceptions are Argentina, South Korea, Germany and Sweden. At the other end of the spectrum, few countries consider the impact of unions and pressure groups as mainly positive; and the USA is the only country that sees religious leaders as a positive force.

Issues surrounding free trade can provoke strong reactions

Attitudes towards major corporations tend to be more positive among developing countries, including China, India and Brazil, than among developed countries such as the USA, Britain and Germany.

Concludes Stewart Lewis:

'The survey's findings demonstrate the apparent dichotomy in developing markets which are both in favour of corporate globalisation and more regulation of large corporations. While socio-political activists in developing markets are hungry for the fruits of corporate globalisation, they may recognise that their justice systems are not sufficiently robust to control the excesses of unfettered corporate growth. Hence, they see a need for greater political regulation of big business.'
13 July 2007

⇨ The above information is reprinted with kind permission from Ipsos MORI. Visit www.ipsos-mori.com for more information.
© Ipsos MORI

KEY FACTS

⇨ Whilst globalisation presents opportunities for all countries it is clear that some countries have benefited more than others. (page 1)

⇨ International trade promotes efficiency and saves resources by encouraging production of goods and services in countries where the costs are lowest. It leads to lower prices for consumers by creating greater competition between businesses. (page 1)

⇨ Global income is more than $40.2 trillion a year, but 19 per cent (1.21 billion) of the world's population earn less than $1 a day. (page 2)

⇨ The digital and information revolution has changed the way the world learns, communicates, does business and treats illnesses. In 2004, there were 545 people per 1000 using the internet in high income countries, while there were only 24 per 1000 in low income countries. (page 2)

⇨ The issues and perceived effects of globalisation excite strong feelings, tempting people to regard it in terms of black and white. (page 3)

⇨ 15% of British people surveyed by the *Financial Times* felt that globalisation was having a positive effect in Great Britain. 53% felt it was having a negative effect, and 32% were not sure. (page 4)

⇨ The average American income is more than 100 times greater than that of a Tanzanian. (page 9)

⇨ The so called 'global village' in reality means that over 1 billion people live on less than $1 a day, with the richest 20% of the world's population consuming over 80% of its resources. (page 13)

⇨ If everyone on earth consumed as much as the average person in the UK, we'd need three planets to support us – and if we consumed as much as the average American, we'd need six planets. (page 13)

⇨ The English spoken in countries with rapidly-booming economies, such as India and China, will increasingly influence this global standard, Linguistics professor David Crystal has said. (page 15)

⇨ The goods we buy in the shops and the materials used to make them come from all over the world and have often been traded many times before we buy them. World trade is currently worth US$7 trillion every year. (page 16)

⇨ Removal of all cotton subsidies and import tariffs would boost global economic welfare by $283 million per year, providing a large benefit to Sub-Saharan Africa, of $147 million per year. (page 18)

⇨ Globalisation has been an important factor in the falling price of manufactured goods. (page 24)

⇨ Globalisation gives an opportunity for domestic firms to export to a wider market. Export-led growth has been an important factor in increasing economic welfare in Asian countries. (page 24)

⇨ Since 1997, DFID has provided nearly £2 million to the Fairtrade Foundation, and is discussing further potential support in the future. DFID wants the Foundation to focus on the poorest producers, assess impact more rigorously, expand the number of people benefiting, have an impact on mainstream supermarkets, and be able to sustain itself financially in the long term. (page 26)

⇨ Fairtrade Labelling Organisations International (FLO) has announced that consumers worldwide spent £1.1bn on Fairtrade Certified Products in 2006. This is a 42% increase on the previous year directly benefiting over 7 million people – farmers, workers and their families in developing countries. (page 30)

⇨ A report from the Adam Smith Institute has claimed that fair trade is unfair. It offers only a very small number of farmers a higher, fixed price for their goods. These higher prices come at the expense of the great majority of farmers, who – unable to qualify for Fairtrade certification – are left even worse off. (page 33)

⇨ 50% of respondents believe that the UK status as a global power is declining while 5% think it is increasing. (page 35)

⇨ The UK public perceive offshoring to be an increasing threat with 82% believing enough jobs have moved offshore already, according to a Deloitte/YouGov survey of attitudes to global economic competition. Just 4% of respondents support the continuation of offshoring. (page 35)

⇨ Britons as a whole are better off with globalisation: consumer goods cost less, and so do mortgages, for example. (page 36)

⇨ The world's most engaged citizens say that while they personally embrace global trade and corporate investment in their homeland, they want their governments to more aggressively crack down on the activities and influence of national and multinational corporations, a new survey reports. (page 39)

GLOSSARY

Capital flight
Money (capital) taken out of a country and re-invested abroad in a safer economy.

Globalisation
Globalisation is an imprecise term used to describe the growing interdependence between countries which is occurring due to the increased flow of trade, communication, services and information around the world. Globalisation is a highly contentious topic, with critics arguing that economic globalisation in particular has widened the gap between rich and poor through unfair trade rules. However, those in favour of globalisation argue that free trade has the potential to lift billions out of poverty, with countries such as China demonstrating through its rapid development the many benefits globalisation can bring.

Global village
The idea that nations are moving closer together and converging into one global community. This is mainly due to increasing global travel and the internet, which has allowed users around the world to connect and communicate. While this brings the advantage of increased understanding and knowledge of cultures and customs around the world, resulting in increased international integration, it can also be seen as a form of colonialism, as Western (and specifically US) culture is imposed on other nations, leading to fears of a global monoculture.

Free trade
An economic policy which promotes the free movement of goods and services between countries and the elimination of restrictions to trading between nations, such as import and export tariffs.

Fair trade
A movement which advocates fair prices, improved working conditions and better trade terms for producers in developing countries. Exports from developing countries that have been certified Fairtrade, which include products such as coffee, cocoa and bananas, carry the Fairtrade mark.

General Agreement on Trade and Tariffs (GATT)
A set of agreements, first signed in 1947, regulating trade between member countries. It was replaced in 1995 by the World Trade Organisation.

Gross Domestic Product (GDP)
The value of all the goods and services produced in a country in a year.

Gross National Product (GNP)
The value of all the goods and services produced by a country in a year, including the income of citizens working abroad.

Interdependence
Interdependent countries are those which are connected to and depend upon each other.

International Monetary Fund (IMF)
An international organisation set up to oversee the global financial system and stabilise exchange rates.

Liberalisation
The relaxation of government restrictions such as barriers to free trade.

Multinational corporations (MNCs)
Powerful companies which operate in more than one country. Due to their size and large economies, multinational corporations – sometimes called trans-national corporations (TNCs) – can hold substantial influence over governments and local economies.

Offshoring
The relocation of business processes from one country to another. Offshoring can reduce business costs and create jobs in developing countries but may also lead to job losses in developed countries.

Protectionism
The policy of protecting domestic industries from foreign competition by restricting trade between nations.

'Sweatshop'
A factory with poor working conditions and low pay where workers are often ill-treated and made to work long hours. Sweatshops are particularly associated with the fashion industry and many companies have been criticised for selling goods produced in this way.

Tariffs
A tax placed on imported and exported goods.

World Bank
An organisation set up to reduce poverty by providing loans for developing countries.

World Trade Organisation (WTO)
An international organisation set up in 1995 to monitor the rules of international trade and promote free trade between countries. The WTO has the power to impose fines or sanctions on member countries that do not follow the rules of trade. Critics of the WTO argue that it holds too much power and protects the interests of rich countries to the disadvantage of developing countries.

INDEX

Additional Resources

Other Issues *titles*

If you are interested in researching further some of the issues raised in *The Problem of Globalisation*, you may like to read the following titles in the **Issues** series:

⇨ Vol. 156 *Travel and Tourism* (ISBN 978 1 86168 443 1)
⇨ Vol. 150 *Migration and Population* (ISBN 978 1 86168 423 3)
⇨ Vol. 134 *Customers and Consumerism* (ISBN 978 1 86168 386 1)
⇨ Vol. 110 *Poverty* (ISBN 978 1 86168 343 3)
⇨ Vol. 104 *Our Internet Society* (ISBN 978 1 86168 324 3)
⇨ Vol. 99 *Exploited Children* (ISBN 978 1 86168 313 7)

For more information about these titles, visit our website at www.independence.co.uk/publicationslist

Useful organisations

You may find the websites of the following organisations useful for further research:

⇨ **De Montfort University:** www.dmu.ac.uk
⇨ **Department for International Development:** www.dfid.gov.uk
⇨ **Economic and Social Research Council:** www.esrcsocietytoday.ac.uk
⇨ **Economics Essays:** www.economicshelp.org
⇨ **Fairtrade Foundation:** www.fairtrade.org.uk
⇨ **Open Democracy:** http://opendemocracy.net
⇨ **Trades Union Congress:** www.tuc.org.uk
⇨ **War on Want:** www.waronwant.org
⇨ **World Development Movement:** www.wdm.org.uk
⇨ **World Trade Organisation:** www.wto.org

ACKNOWLEDGEMENTS

The publisher is grateful for permission to reproduce the following material.

While every care has been taken to trace and acknowledge copyright, the publisher tenders its apology for any accidental infringement or where copyright has proved untraceable. The publisher would be pleased to come to a suitable arrangement in any such case with the rightful owner.

Chapter One: Overview

What is globalisation?, © Crown copyright is reproduced with the permission of Her Majesty's Stationery Office, *Globalisation explained*, © Economic and Social Research Council, *Globalisation defined*, © Trades Union Congress, *A globalisation glossary*, © De Montfort University, *Concerns about globalisation*, © Crown copyright is reproduced with the permission of Her Majesty's Stationery Office, *The Bretton Woods Institutions*, © Bretton Woods Project, *Globalisation – problems and solutions*, © The Big Green Footprint, *Making the global village a reality*, © Guardian Newspapers Ltd, *English will fragment into 'global dialects'*, © Telegraph Group Ltd.

Chapter Two: Globalisation and Trade

World trade, © National Youth Agency, *Trade – did you know?*, © Crown copyright is reproduced with the permission of Her Majesty's Stationery Office, *Trade and the WTO*, © War on Want, *The WTO – 10 common misunderstandings*, © World Trade Organisation, *Globalisation and the poor*, © Economics Essays, *Examples of unfair trade rules*, © World Development Movement, *Fighting poverty through trade*, © Crown copyright is reproduced with the permission of Her Majesty's Stationery Office, *'Sweatshops shame' fashion alert*, © War on Want, *Sweat, fire and ethics*, © New Internationalist, *Globalisation and multinationals*, © The Business, *The fairtrade boom*, © Fairtrade Foundation, *'Teach us how to fish – do not just give is the fish'*, © Guardian newspapers Ltd, *Unfair trade?*, © Adam Smith Institute, *Globalisation will not threaten skilled UK workers*, © Personnel Today, *Offshoring and UK workers*, © Deloitte and Touche LLP, *Britain and globalisation: a good marriage*, © Open Democracy, *Making globalisation work*, © Project Syndicate/ Institute for Human Sciences, *Attitudes to global trade*, © Ipsos MORI.

Photographs

Lisa Firth: page 11.
Flickr: pages 13 (Guy Freeman); 17 (Refracted Moments™); 23 (Dave Morris); 26 (Labour behind the label); 32 (Peter Mulligan); 39 (b.wu).
Stock Xchng: pages 1 (Barun Patro); 3 (Sanja Gjenero); 7 (Steve Woods); 18 (Pam Roth); 19 (ArtMechanic); 30 (pachd); 34 (Ralph Morris).

Illustrations

Pages 2, 14, 29: Don Hatcher; pages 6, 16, 36: Simon Kneebone; pages 8, 20, 38: Angelo Madrid; pages 12, 25: Bev Aisbett.

Research and glossary by Claire Owen, with additional by Lisa Firth, on behalf of Independence Educational Publishers.

Additional editorial by Claire Owen, on behalf of Independence Educational Publishers.

And with thanks to the team: Mary Chapman, Sandra Dennis, Claire Owen and Jan Sunderland.

Lisa Firth
Cambridge
April, 2008